ECONOMIC ISSUES, PROBLEMS AND PERSPECTIVES

U.S. CURRENCY AND THE BLIND AND VISUALLY IMPAIRED

ADDRESSING ACCESSIBILITY FEATURES

ECONOMIC ISSUES, PROBLEMS AND PERSPECTIVES

Additional books in this series can be found on Nova's website
under the Series tab.

Additional e-books in this series can be found on Nova's website
under the e-book tab.

ECONOMIC ISSUES, PROBLEMS AND PERSPECTIVES

U.S. CURRENCY AND THE BLIND AND VISUALLY IMPAIRED

ADDRESSING ACCESSIBILITY FEATURES

ARLENE TRUMAN
EDITOR

nova publishers
New York

Library of Congress Cataloging-in-Publication Data

ISBN: 978-1-63463-903-3

Published by Nova Science Publishers, Inc. † New York

CONTENTS

PREFACE

This book examines the status of BEP's efforts to provide currency that is accessible for visually impaired persons and how BEP is considering costs as part of these efforts; and factors that may affect BEP's efforts.

Chapter 1 – All blind and many persons with low vision are unable to distinguish currency denominations without assistance. The U.S. District Court for the District of Columbia found that Treasury failed to provide meaningful access to U.S. currency to visually impaired persons, and in 2008, ordered Treasury to take steps to do so. The court did not define meaningful access, leaving it to Treasury to choose a course of action. Within Treasury, BEP designs and manufactures currency. GAO was asked to review the progress BEP has made toward meeting the district court's order. In addition, the Explanatory Statement accompanying the Consolidated Appropriations Act, 2014, mandated GAO to report on strategies for minimizing the cost of developing currency with accessibility features.

This report examines (1) the status of BEP's efforts to provide currency that is accessible for visually impaired persons and how BEP is considering costs as part of these efforts and (2) factors that may affect BEP's efforts. To answer these questions GAO reviewed court and BEP documents, and interviewed officials from BEP, the Federal Reserve Board, and the Secret Service as well as representatives from advocacy organizations for visually impaired persons and trade associations for cash-handling companies.

Chapter 2 – The mission of the Bureau of Engraving and Printing (BEP) is to develop and produce U.S. currency (Federal Reserve notes) that is trusted worldwide. As its primary function, the BEP prints approximately 6.5 to 8.5 billion Federal Reserve notes each year depending on an annual order from the Board of Governors of the Federal Reserve System (the Board). As the issuing authority, the Board takes delivery of the Federal Reserve notes from the BEP and issues them to the Federal Reserve Banks which, in turn, distribute them to the public through depository institutions that have a Federal Reserve account.

In June 2012, the Senate Committee on Appropriations issued Senate Report 112-177. This report directed "the BEP to report to Congress and to Treasury's Office of Inspector General (OIG) within 90 days of enactment [the 2013 Financial Services and General Government Appropriations bill] on a detailed plan, including a timeline, to develop, design, test, and print currency with accessibility features. The plan should also include an analysis of the feasibility of expediting the Federal acquisition process for the specialized equipment required to create accessibility features. The Committee directs the OIG to provide an initial assessment of the plan to the Committee within 60 days of receipt and to report on its progress and implementation every 6 months thereafter until the plan is fully implemented." Although the legislation accompanying the Senate Report was not enacted, given the high level of interest, and to enhance communication and openness, the BEP is submitting this white paper to the Treasury OIG and the Senate Committee on Appropriations.

Chapter 3 – The Bureau of Engraving and Printing (BEP), a bureau within the United States (U.S.) Department of the Treasury, is responsible for designing and producing the U.S. Federal Reserve notes (hereafter referred to as U.S. currency). The BEP initiated this study to examine various aspects of the use of U.S. currency by the blind and visually impaired (VI) population of the U.S. The data, research, and analysis presented in this study will be used to evaluate potential measures that may enhance or improve the ability of the blind and VI to identify currency denominations. Many factors impact the BEP's flexibility in modifying U.S. currency. The BEP must balance printing efficiency, counterfeit deterrence features, statutory requirements, and general banknote aesthetics when it determines a banknote's design to better serve the needs of those who are blind or visually impaired. All of these factors play a vital role in currency design. While this study does not make recommendations, it does provide data regarding future design of U.S. currency that will be useful to the BEP in making such recommendations in the future.

The BEP has engaged ARINC Engineering Services, LLC, an ARINC company, hereafter referred to as ARINC, to conduct a study addressing options for improving the ability of the blind and VI community to denominate[1] U.S. currency. For purposes of this study, ARINC established an "ARINC team" to perform this study through subcontracts with Battelle Memorial Institute, Naois LLC, and the University of Maine. Of note, all ARINC team members are independent from any security paper industry producers and original equipment manufacturers, including hand-held electronic readers, currency raw material or equipment suppliers, or any BEP service providers.

In: U.S. Currency and the Blind and Visually Impaired   ISBN: 978-1-63463-903-3
Editor: Arlene Truman   © 2015 Nova Science Publishers, Inc.

Chapter 1

U.S. CURRENCY: READER PROGRAM SHOULD BE EVALUATED WHILE OTHER ACCESSIBILITY FEATURES FOR VISUALLY IMPAIRED PERSONS ARE DEVELOPED[*]

United States Government Accountability Office

ABBREVIATIONS

ACB	American Council of the Blind
ACD	Advanced Counterfeit Deterrence Steering Committee
BEP	Bureau of Engraving and Printing
CQA	Currency Quality Assurance program
ICD	Interagency Currency Design Group
NLS	National Library Services for the Blind and Physically Handicapped
PAC	Program Approval Committee

WHY GAO DID THIS STUDY

All blind and many persons with low vision are unable to distinguish currency denominations without assistance. The U.S. District Court for the District of Columbia found that Treasury failed to provide meaningful access to U.S. currency to visually impaired persons, and in 2008, ordered Treasury to take steps to do so. The court did not define meaningful access, leaving it to Treasury to choose a course of action. Within Treasury, BEP designs and manufactures currency. GAO was asked to review the progress BEP has made toward meeting the district court's order. In addition, the Explanatory Statement

---

[*] This is an edited, reformatted and augmented version of The United States Government Accountability Office publication, GAO-14-823, dated September 2014.

accompanying the Consolidated Appropriations Act, 2014, mandated GAO to report on strategies for minimizing the cost of developing currency with accessibility features.

This report examines (1) the status of BEP's efforts to provide currency that is accessible for visually impaired persons and how BEP is considering costs as part of these efforts and (2) factors that may affect BEP's efforts. To answer these questions GAO reviewed court and BEP documents, and interviewed officials from BEP, the Federal Reserve Board, and the Secret Service as well as representatives from advocacy organizations for visually impaired persons and trade associations for cash-handling companies.

WHAT GAO RECOMMENDS

GAO recommends BEP evaluate its currency reader program while it develops a tactile feature in the next redesign of currency. BEP did not take a position on our recommendation.

WHAT GAO FOUND

The Bureau of Engraving and Printing (BEP) has progressed in making currency accessible through a three-pronged approach it adopted and is considering the costs of its approach as it continues its efforts. BEP has:

- Added large, high-contrast numerals to notes, and it plans to continue to refine these numerals.
- Started to distribute free currency-reader devices that can scan a note and audibly announce its value. However, BEP's plans to evaluate the effectiveness of this new program are incomplete, and without a complete evaluation, BEP cannot determine the program's effectiveness.
- Made limited progress in developing a raised tactile feature on notes, which would provide the ability to determine the note's value by touch. While BEP has narrowed the options of what a tactile feature would look like on a note and how it would be applied, BEP officials stated that challenges developing the feature will delay selecting an option to test until March 2015—over a year behind schedule.

Supplementing these efforts, BEP developed a smartphone app that identifies notes. High-contrast numerals add little additional cost, and BEP estimates it will spend about $35 million on currency readers over 3 years. Cost estimates to produce a tactile feature are preliminary and range widely.

GAO identified three factors that may affect BEP's efforts to complete its three-pronged approach. First, the inclusion of a tactile feature will require a redesign of currency, but it is not known when this will occur. Because BEP makes changes to currency to stay ahead of counterfeit threats, redesign occurs as needed and not at regular intervals. Second, BEP has faced difficulties developing a raised tactile feature, falling behind its internal schedule. Third, senior BEP and Federal Reserve officials told us that they have discussed the Federal

Reserve's concerns about the potential cost impact of a tactile feature and whether technological changes since the 2008 court order could provide alternative options to BEP's current approach. BEP officials stated that they have not yet determined how these concerns might be addressed. Advocates for organizations representing visually impaired persons consider a tactile feature to be important and are concerned about the length of time it is taking BEP to provide access to currency.

Large, High-Contrast Numeral and Currency Reader Device

Sources: U.S. Bureau of Engravingand Printing and GAO. GAO-14-823.

* * *

September 26, 2014

Congressional Committees

All blind and many persons with low vision[1] are unable to distinguish one denomination of U.S. currency[2] from another without assistance because the notes are uniform in size, texture, and general design. To identify the value of a note, a blind person must rely on a sighted person for help or use an assistive device that can identify a note and signal its value audibly or by vibrating. A person with low vision may likewise require assistance in some circumstances—such as in low lighting—but may be able to identify note denominations in other circumstances. The inability to consistently distinguish the value of notes without external help, according to a 1995 National Research Council study[3] and advocates for the visually impaired, prevents visually impaired individuals from fully participating in society because they cannot independently and confidentially exchange currency, such as when making cash purchases or using public transportation.[4]

The American Council of the Blind (ACB) and two individuals brought suit against the Department of the Treasury (Treasury) in 2002, alleging that it discriminates against visually impaired persons by not providing readily identifiable U.S. currency.[5] In 2006, the U.S. District Court for the District of Columbia found that Treasury failed to provide "meaningful access" to U.S. currency to visually impaired persons[6] and, in 2008, the court ordered Treasury to take steps to provide meaningful access.[7] Within Treasury, the Bureau of Engraving and Printing (BEP) designs and manufactures U.S. currency.[8]

The Senate report accompanying the Financial Services and General Government Appropriations Act, included as division E of the Consolidated Appropriations Act, 2014, mandated us to review how BEP can expedite the development, design, testing, and printing of currency with accessibility features. In addition, the Explanatory Statement accompanying the Consolidated Appropriations Act, 2014, mandated us to report on strategies for minimizing the cost of developing currency with accessibility features. Subsequently, Senator Murray asked us to review the progress BEP has made toward meeting the district court's 2008 order. This report examines

1. the status of BEP's efforts to provide currency that is accessible for visually impaired persons and how BEP is considering costs as part of these efforts, and
2. factors that may affect BEP's efforts to make currency accessible for visually impaired persons.

To gather information on both objectives, we reviewed agency documents related to BEP's efforts to provide currency that is accessible.

Specifically, we reviewed documents related to the 2002 court case and BEP's semi-annual progress reports to the court. We interviewed officials from the three agencies that work together to redesign currency: BEP, the Board of Governors of the Federal Reserve System (Federal Reserve), and the United States Secret Service (Secret Service). In addition, to identify and discuss the factors that may affect BEP's approach to make currency accessible for visually impaired persons, we interviewed representatives of four national advocacy organizations for visually impaired persons and four trade associations that represent financial institutions and other companies that use cash-handling equipment, such as ATM manufacturers. We also interviewed Bank of Canada representatives because of their efforts to produce accessible currency. The results of the interviews are not generalizable, but do provide insights regarding efforts to make currency accessible to blind and visually impaired persons. See appendix I for additional information on our scope and methodology.

We conducted this performance audit from February 2014 to September 2014 in accordance with generally accepted government auditing standards. Those standards require that we plan and perform the audit to obtain sufficient, appropriate evidence to provide a reasonable basis for our findings and conclusions based on our audit objectives. We believe that the evidence obtained provides a reasonable basis for our findings and conclusions based on our audit objectives.

BACKGROUND

According to estimates from several sources, approximately 8 to 12 million Americans live with some type of visual impairment, including 300,000 to 1.3 million who are blind.[9] Impairment can range from individuals with limited vision that is not correctable by glasses or contact lenses to those who are not able to perceive objects at any distance.[10]

The number of Americans with some type of visual impairment is projected to increase as the population ages. One of the leading causes of vision loss is disease, such as glaucoma, cataracts, and diabetes. Some individuals who suffer vision loss suffer physical ailments; for example, individuals with diabetes can suffer both vision loss and a loss of feeling in their fingers. Birth defects and accidents also can cause vision loss, and veterans may have vision loss from wounds or trauma.

Currencies of most other countries have characteristics that make their notes accessible to visually impaired persons.[11] Most commonly, countries use different-sized notes and color to distinguish different denominations. Among nine major foreign countries surveyed by economists at the Federal Reserve Bank of St. Louis, eight used those two features in their currency. In addition, all nine used a tactile feature[12] or large, high-contrast numerals, or both. For example, the European Union uses different-sized notes, different primary colors for each denomination, and large numerals. The €200 and €500 notes also include a tactile feature. Canada has incorporated a raised tactile feature in its currency since 2001 and uses different colors and large, high-contrast numerals. Federal Reserve officials we spoke with noted that the existence of accessible features does not necessarily mean these features are effective. For example, they said that they have been unable to identify a tactile feature used by another country that remains effective for the life of the note.

In the Order and Judgment reflecting the court's decision in the ACB lawsuit, the court did not specifically define meaningful access and left it to the discretion of the Secretary of the Treasury as to how to fulfill the requirement of the court order. The court required Treasury to provide meaningful access no later than the date of the next currency redesign for each of the denominations. [13] The order also requires Treasury to submit semi-annual reports so that the court can monitor Treasury's progress. The order remains in effect until Treasury fulfills the requirement.

In 2010, BEP proposed a three-pronged approach[14] consisting of three elements it believes will provide meaningful access to currency: 1) large, high-contrast numerals to allow low vision individuals to determine the denomination of currency, 2) currency readers that can indicate a note's value,[15] and 3) a raised tactile feature to allow visually impaired persons to denominate currency by touch. According to BEP, it chose this approach because no single solution would enable all segments of the diverse visually impaired population to denominate currency with 100 percent accuracy. BEP also stated in a 2010 Federal Register notice on its proposed approach that it would explore emerging technological options to provide access to currency, such as smartphone applications that can act as a currency reader.[16] In 2011, the Treasury submitted its three-pronged approach and a plan to explore emerging technologies to the court. Each of the elements of BEP's approach is discussed further in the next section of this report.

Table 1. Federal Agencies with Responsibilities for U.S. Currency

Federal Agency	Responsibility
Bureau of Engraving and Printing	BEP designs and is the sole producer of U.S. paper currency.
Board of Governors of the Federal Reserve System	As the central bank for the United States, the Federal Reserve has the sole authority to issue currency. The Federal Reserve orders currency from BEP and pays BEP for its currency-related expenses.
U.S. Secret Service[a]	The Secret Service conducts investigations of counterfeiting activities and provides counterfeit-detection training as part of its mission to safeguard the nation's financial infrastructure.

Source: GAO analysis. | GAO-14-823.

[a]The Secret Service is a component of the Department of Homeland Security.

Two elements of BEP's approach—large, high-contrast numerals and a tactile feature—require changes to the design of the currency. Making such changes to currency is a complex and lengthy process, involving three agencies: BEP, the Federal Reserve, and the Secret Service (see table 1).

According to BEP documents, these agencies work together through an interagency governance structure, which includes the following committees: [17]

- Advanced Counterfeit Deterrence Steering Committee (ACD): Comprised of senior-level officials, the ACD is empowered to make recommendations on note design, production, and security to the Secretary of the Treasury, who approves the final currency design.
- Interagency Currency Design Group (ICD): The ICD is chartered to initiate, authorize, and prioritize interagency activities related to note redesign and production. The ICD provides a management framework for the note redesign process and makes recommendations to the ACD.

Program Approval Committee (PAC): The PAC consists of a subset of ICD members. It is chartered to provide oversight and direction to all note-redesign projects. In that capacity, it reviews and approves recommendations from project teams. It also provides a forum for members to inquire about project details and resource prioritization.

The United States has had two major redesigns of its currency since the 1930s.[18] Each redesign involved changes to a family of notes—the $5, $10, $20, $50 and $100 notes—and included design elements required by statute as well as features to deter new counterfeit threats.[19] Under current law, the Department of the Treasury is not permitted to use appropriated funds to redesign the $1 note.[20] Redesigned notes retained familiar characteristics of the notes they replaced, but included new features or new versions of existing features that make each note distinct. For example, while the size and location of the portrait on a note changed, the portrait is of the same person. Figure 1 shows different versions of portraits on the $100 note.

Note issued beginning in 1996   Note issued beginning in 2013

Sources: U.S. Bureau of Engravingand Printing and GAO. GAO-14-823.

Figure 1. Differences between Portraits on 1996 and 2013 $100 Notes.

BEP has increasingly used distinctive features to enhance a note's appearance and resistance to counterfeiting. For example, BEP added a series of individual features known as symbols of freedom to notes, such as two images of the Statue of Liberty's torch on the $10 note. Security features, like the bell in the inkwell on the most recent $100 note,[21] make it easier for the public to identify an authentic note and are difficult for counterfeiters to reproduce. The development of these individual and security features occurs separately from the overall design of the note, which includes the note layout and artwork. Once the features and the overall design receive interagency approval, they are combined to achieve a final product. The length of time required to redesign a note depends mostly on the length of time it takes to research, develop, and test new security features. For example, BEP spent nearly 10 years developing security features for the most recent $100 note. Developing individual features involves a less rigorous process because BEP does not rely on them for counterfeit protection. The redesign process may also be lengthened if the Secret Service, the Federal Reserve, or industry members, such as banks, identify problems with the test notes they receive before full production. If there is a problem with the test notes, such as if notes do not function correctly in the automated high-speed currency-counting equipment used by the Federal Reserve and many banks, the design of a note would need to be adjusted and resubmitted for interagency review. Although the development of features and the development of the overall design use separate processes, agency officials said that information is shared between the processes on an ongoing basis. Figure 2 describes the steps in the development processes for a redesigned note and an individual feature. The raised tactile feature BEP plans to add to currency is following the process BEP uses for developing an individual feature.

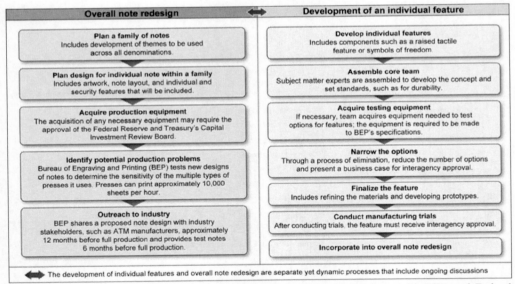

Source: GAO analysis of BEP and Federal Reserve information, interwiews with BEP and Federal Reserve officials and GAO. GAO-14-823.

Figure 2. Steps Involved in Note Redesign.

The Federal Reserve determines when newly redesigned notes are placed into circulation based on the needs of the Federal Reserve Banks and depository institutions. As a result, there may be some time between when a redesigned note is produced by BEP and when it enters circulation. After redesigned notes enter circulation, they co-circulate with the previously designed notes for many years because of the notes' longevity. For example, the Federal Reserve estimates that a $5 note remains in circulation for almost 5 years and a $100 note for 15 years. The newest redesigned note, the $100, began entering circulation in 2013.

BEP HAS TAKEN ACTIONS TO MAKE CURRENCY ACCESSIBLE AND IS CONSIDERING COSTS AS IT CONTINUES ITS EFFORTS

BEP Has Made Some Progress Implementing Its Three-Pronged Approach

BEP has taken steps to make currency accessible to visually impaired persons, but has not yet fully implemented any element of its three-pronged approach. Specifically, BEP is producing some notes with large, high-contrast numerals, has begun the initial phases of the currency reader program, and is conducting research for a raised tactile feature. In addition to these efforts, BEP has also developed an application for smartphones that can be used to identify the value of notes. According to BEP officials, as of May 2014, they were in the process of design planning activities for the next family of notes. Figure 3 shows a timeline of events related to the court case and currency redesign.

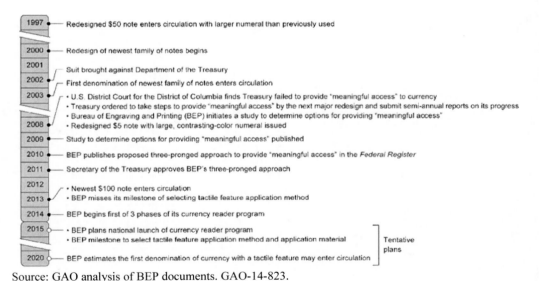

Source: GAO analysis of BEP documents. GAO-14-823.

Figure 3. Timeline of Select Events Relevant to BEP's Efforts to Make Currency Accessible.

Large, High-Contrast Numerals
From 1997 to 2008, BEP added larger numerals to the backs of all notes it redesigned except the $1 and $2 notes, and from 2008 to 2013, BEP included even larger, colored

numerals in the designs of the $5 and $100 notes. The numerals are primarily designed to allow persons with low vision to independently denominate a note. According to BEP, it will continue to use high-contrast numerals in future currency redesigns and is exploring ways to refine the numerals, including options concerning attributes such as size, color, placement, and background contrast for large numerals. Figure 4 shows notes before and after BEP added larger numerals.

$50 banknote issued beginning in 1990 without large numerals.

$50 banknote issued beginning in 1997 with larger, high-contrast numeral on the lower right corner.

$5 banknote issued beginning in 2008 with large, purple numeral.

$100 banknote issued beginning in 2013 with large, gold numeral.

Source: U.S. Bureau of Engraving and Printing and GAO. GAO-14-823.

Figure 4. Select U.S. Notes Showing Changes to Numerals.

Advocates for visually impaired persons have been circumspect in their response to the addition of large, high-contrast numerals. The representatives stated they are supportive of the numerals because they assist a portion of the visually impaired population. However, the representatives noted that the benefit of large, high-contrast numerals is dependent upon the amount of useful vision a person has and the lighting in the environment. In addition, representatives told us that high-contrast numerals alone are not sufficient to provide visually impaired persons access to currency.

Currency Reader Device Program

BEP began the first of the three phases of its currency reader program in July 2014. In the first phase, BEP distributed free reader devices to eligible persons at the annual conferences of three national organizations for visually impaired persons. In the second phase, to start in September 2014, existing participants of the Library of Congress' National Library Services for the Blind and Physically Handicapped (NLS) are to be eligible to pre-order a currency reader. NLS, through an interagency agreement with BEP, is to determine applicants' eligibility for free readers, process orders, and ship currency readers as a supplement to its existing service of providing braille and audio materials free to qualified participants. For the final phase, BEP anticipates a national rollout of its program in January 2015, with plans to make reader devices available to any eligible person. In June 2014, BEP's Director said he projects distributing between 100,000 and 500,000 readers over 3 years. According to BEP officials, they distributed about 1,600 devices at the three annual conferences.[22]

The reader device, known as the iBill and shown in figure 5, is battery-operated, about 1.6 inches by 3 inches in size, and includes an earphone jack for privacy. To denominate a note, a user inserts a U.S. note of any denomination between $1 and $100 into the slot, under the raised portion of the front of the reader, and presses and releases a button. According to BEP, the reader will identify most notes within one second, although notes in poor condition may require more time.[23] To indicate the denomination of a note, the reader can announce the denomination out loud in English, emit a varying number of beeps and pitches, or vibrate for a varying number of pulses and durations. For example, the reader can indicate a $20 note by announcing "Twenty," emitting two high-pitched beeps, or vibrating for two long pulses.

Source: U.S. Bureau of Engraving and Printing and GAO. GAO-14-823.

Figure 5. Currency Reader Device That the Bureau of Engraving and Printing (BEP) Provides to Visually Impaired Persons.

According to the BEP Director, the currency reader program is a key part of BEP's three-pronged approach to provide access to currency, and is designed as the one method that can provide virtually all visually impaired persons with a means to independently denominate notes. BEP projects spending about $35 million on the currency reader program over the next 3 years. The need for currency readers will likely continue for many years because BEP estimates the first note with a tactile feature will not likely be issued before 2020. BEP expects future notes to be issued, as they have historically been, one denomination at a time over several years and expects that notes without tactile features will co-circulate with tactile-enhanced notes for many years.

BEP officials described steps they have taken, or plan to take, to evaluate the currency reader program's effectiveness. For example, they solicited feedback from the organizations for visually impaired and their members and established a toll-free phone number for people to call with questions or concerns about the program or address issues or problems with devices. While these efforts are useful, they are incomplete because they do not provide BEP information on other aspects of the currency reader program. For example, BEP does not plan to evaluate how well the program provides visually impaired persons with a means to independently denominate currency. Further, BEP does not plan to evaluate program costs or time frames, even though BEP anticipates spending tens of millions of dollars for many years. According to BEP officials, BEP has been focused on implementing the program instead of evaluating it. GAO's prior work on federal agencies that have used program evaluation for decision making has shown that program evaluation can allow agencies to understand whether a program is addressing the problem it is intended to and assess the value or effectiveness of the program.[24] The results of an evaluation can be used to clarify BEP and others' understanding of how the program does or does not address a problem of interest and to assist BEP in making changes to improve the design or management of an existing program. Without such an evaluation, BEP cannot determine whether the currency reader program is reaching users as intended and providing them with appropriate access to currency.

In general, advocates for visually impaired persons support the currency reader program because it can help some members of the visually impaired community. However, some advocates pointed out that many people who are visually impaired carry several assistive devices, such as a cane or magnification devices. A currency reader requires a visually impaired person to carry an additional device, which can be cumbersome. For example, representatives from one organization stated that it would be difficult for a person to hold a wallet, banknotes, and a currency reader device to determine the denomination of a note. In addition, some advocates told us that because of the time it takes to use a reader, the device does not enable a visually impaired person to identify notes as quickly and easily as a tactile feature. Representatives from two advocacy organizations told us their members had mixed reactions to the currency reader devices distributed at the annual conferences. One group noted problems with some of the devices, such as not reading notes properly and announcing an error message even when it was not being used, while the other group reported that members seemed satisfied.

Raised Tactile Feature

BEP has evaluated a range of potential raised tactile features but has not received final interagency approval for a feature or for its characteristics, such as its shape, denominating pattern,[25] and location on each note. A raised tactile feature is one that is applied to the surface of a note and offers a contrasting feel compared to the surface around it.[26] A BEP core team of subject matter experts has not yet determined how to apply the feature to notes, and it did not meet a key, internal milestone. According to BEP's timeline, selection of the application method, or process it will use to create the raised tactile feature on the surface of the note, was due to be finalized by December 2013. The tactile feature core team researched and analyzed many potential application methods, narrowed the choices to four for further analysis, and recommended one to the interagency PAC based on that further analysis. BEP must receive interagency approval from the PAC on its chosen application method in order to finalize its selection.

The core team presented its recommended application method to the PAC in March 2014, but the PAC did not approve it because of concerns about the analysis used to test and compare the application methods. For example, BEP set a requirement that a raised tactile feature allow a person to accurately identify a note's denomination in less than 30 seconds. The PAC noted, however, that the core team used a different time interval when testing the application methods. The PAC directed the core team to update the requirements for the tactile feature and revise the test methods used to ensure they address the updated requirements. BEP now anticipates selecting an application method by March 2015, which would put it over one year behind its tactile feature development schedule.

Although BEP has not received final approval for other feature characteristics, it received interagency approval for a design of the tactile feature's appearance and denominating pattern for use in testing and comparing application methods. BEP determined that a raised tactile feature shaped as a 6mm x 4mm rectangle would be highly perceptible to touch, compared to a range of other shapes.[27] BEP also determined the pattern that would be used on each denomination, as shown in figure 6, but not where the feature would be located on a note.

Source: GAO. GAO-14-823.

Figure 6. Raised Tactile Feature Design and Denominating Pattern Approved for Use in Testing.

Advocates for visually impaired persons told us that a tactile feature would allow visually impaired persons to quickly determine the value of each note without assistance and decrease their vulnerability in many situations. Representatives from ACB said that physical changes to a note, such as a tactile feature, are a sure way to provide independence for visually impaired persons. In July 2014, ACB passed a resolution reiterating the importance of not delaying the production of currency that is accessible to visually impaired persons.

Emerging Technological Options

In addition to the three-pronged approach approved by the Secretary of the Treasury, BEP developed an application (app) for Apple's iOS operating system and contributed to the development of an app for Google's Android operating system. According to BEP, the Apple iOS app was intended to immediately provide a segment of the visually impaired population with a means to independently denominate notes, while a tactile feature was being developed. Officials stated that BEP will maintain the app as long as it continues to be used.

In 2010, BEP developed an Apple iOS operating system app, called EyeNote, which is available as a free download. Because of technology changes to smart phones, BEP released a new version in 2013. In the newest version, once the downloaded app is launched, the app continually scans for a note and can identify any denomination between $1 and $100 using either the front or back of the note. It either announces the denomination in English or Spanish or announces the denomination by varying a number of beeps or vibration pulses, depending on the device used. For example, a $20 note is announced as five vibrations on the Apple iPhone. As of August 2014 the app has been downloaded over 18,000 times. BEP also worked with the Department of Education on the development of a comparable free app for the Android operating system, called IDEAL Currency Identifier, which was released in 2012 and updated in 2014.

BEP Is Considering Costs As It Implements Its Three-pronged Approach

Advocates for visually impaired persons said that while smart phones and therefore smart phone applications can be useful, they are not widely used among all groups of visually impaired persons, in part because of their high cost. Some representatives said that as with the currency reader device, an app is not beneficial in all situations and still requires the user to take the time to open the app, scan the note, and hear the app's announcement.

We identified examples of how BEP considers costs and ways to manage them as it implements its three-pronged approach and pursues emerging technologies to provide access to currency for visually impaired persons. BEP is in different stages of implementing each element of its approach, and cost is considered in different ways for each.

Large, High-Contrast Numerals

According to BEP officials, including large, high-contrast numerals to previous note designs added almost no cost to BEP, and the officials anticipate the same for the next redesign. There was no additional cost for special inks because BEP used the same inks that were already incorporated into other features.

Currency Reader Program

BEP leveraged existing resources to manage costs for the currency reader device program. For example, in 2013, it signed an agreement with the NLS to determine eligibility and fulfill orders for currency readers. NLS has an existing process for qualifying blind and visually impaired individuals for eligibility to receive free braille and audio material and an established infrastructure for processing customer orders and for warehousing and shipping materials to individuals. BEP estimates that the cost of the services provided by NLS will be approximately $1.8 million through the end of fiscal year 2015. BEP also took steps, when purchasing currency readers, to constrain costs or limit the risk of excess cost. For example, BEP conducted an open solicitation to ensure a competitive procurement and sought to purchase commercially available reader devices. BEP's 3-year fixed-price contract to purchase readers, which sets a per-unit cost for each year, provides flexibility in the number of devices BEP orders because it does not know the exact number of currency readers needed. The contract also requires the supplier to provide the readers in packaging ready for shipping that meets all U.S. Postal Service standards for "Free Matter," so BEP does not incur additional cost to prepare or ship the devices.[28]

Raised Tactile Feature

Because BEP has not determined how it will apply a tactile feature to notes, it does not have final current estimates of the costs to produce currency with a tactile feature. Instead, BEP developed cost estimates for each of the four potential tactile feature application methods it was considering.[29] According to BEP, most of the internal costs for a new feature like the raised tactile feature are associated with acquisition and modification of needed manufacturing equipment. Estimates for these non-recurring costs range from $1.1 million for one application method to about $85 million for each of the other three.[30] Estimates for recurring costs of each application method range from $9.7 million to $14.4 million annually.

BEP also sought to estimate potential costs to the Federal Reserve and cash-handling industry, including armored carriers, banks, and banknote equipment manufacturers.[31] However, BEP was not able to do so because it found that the potential costs to the Federal Reserve and industry are dependent on the height of the tactile feature, which has not been determined. BEP obtained information from the ATM industry on the potential impact of an added tactile feature. The industry estimated a range of $1.3 billion to $1.8 billion for non-recurring equipment changes to ATMs and a range of $600 million to $3.4 billion for increased annual transportation costs.[32] A representative of the ATM industry told us that the industry cannot make reasonable estimates until BEP announces the specific height and application method of the tactile feature. However, banking and ATM industry representatives also said that they will accommodate changes to currency if they are provided sufficient time to prepare.

Emerging Technological Options

In addition to the costs for its three-pronged approach, BEP has additional costs for the development and maintenance of its EyeNote app. BEP contracted with a developer for the initial development and project management of the EyeNote. Officials stated that the cost of the first version of the app was $550,000 and the newest version was $250,000. BEP will pay an annual maintenance cost of approximately $35,000 to the developer beginning in December 2014.

THREE FACTORS THAT COULD AFFECT BEP'S CURRENT EFFORTS

Currency Is Redesigned to Prevent Counterfeit

According to senior Federal Reserve and BEP officials, currency redesign primarily occurs in response to counterfeit threats and does not occur at specific intervals. As a result, it is unknown when the next redesign will occur. The ACD makes recommendations to the Secretary of the Treasury on when to redesign currency based on counterfeit threat analyses; the Secretary has the sole authority to approve note design. The Chair of the Federal Reserve determines when a redesigned note will be placed in circulation. In a 2013 report submitted to the court, BEP estimated that a new note with a tactile feature would commence circulation in 2020. In 2014 testimony, the BEP's Director stated that a note with a tactile feature would not be introduced before 2020. However, Federal Reserve officials stated that the date has not received interagency approval.

BEP's need to address identified counterfeit threats could affect the redesign process. BEP officials told us they are continuously developing security features to stay ahead of counterfeiters. As previously discussed, the length of time for redesign is, in part, dependent on sufficient security features approved through the interagency process. Large, high-contrast numerals and a tactile feature are not considered security features that would be used in response to counterfeit threats.

Representatives from organizations that advocate for visually impaired persons expressed concern about the length of time it is taking BEP to provide access to currency. Specifically, during the court case, Treasury stated that currency redesign occurs approximately every 7 to 10 years. Because the court order was issued in 2008, the advocacy representatives expected the next redesign of currency to be issued beginning in approximately 2015 to 2018. There is no approved date for the introduction of redesigned currency with a tactile feature.

BEP Has Experienced Challenges Developing a Raised Tactile Feature

Why Can't a Tactile Feature Be Added Now?

A tactile feature is only effective if it is perceptible, meaning that it is easy to differentiate it from the texture of the area around the feature. There is no space on any current denomination that would suffice to provide the perceptibility. Because banknotes already include some raised printing and have overt and covert security features, the introduction of a tactile feature could interfere with the other features. As a result, the introduction of a tactile feature would require a major currency redesign.

Source: GAO analysis of BEP documents and interviews with BEP officials. | GAO-14-823.

BEP has faced difficulties developing a raised tactile feature, and it has fallen behind its estimated schedule. Developing a durable-raised tactile feature has proved challenging internationally and for BEP. A 2009 study BEP commissioned showed that the tactility of features used by several other countries diminishes over time as the notes circulate.[33] BEP has not developed a raised tactile feature before, so it had to create an internal structure and process for testing and evaluating potential features. Officials stated that BEP had to test some options for application methods externally because it did not have the equipment. This lack of equipment lengthened the time to make a recommendation on an application method. As discussed previously, BEP did not make a recommendation until 3 months after its milestone date of December 2013. According to BEP, it now anticipates finalizing an application method, which is needed to move forward on a tactile feature, by March 2015.

BEP has had challenges in the past with the design and production of new features, challenges that have led to significant changes to BEP's processes. Specifically, in 2010 BEP began producing the new $100 note, which included, among other new features, a plastic 3-D security ribbon woven into the paper. This composite of paper and plastic is unlike any other denomination of U.S. currency. After full production began, BEP officials found creases in some of the notes. The creasing occurred on a sufficient number of notes that BEP suspended production 9 months after it had started. Testing found that there were several contributing factors, including the paper's moisture content, the amount of recycled material in the paper, and the amount of time between paper manufacture and printing. However, BEP did not discover these problems until over a year after the problem occurred. The Treasury Inspector General determined that BEP did not sufficiently validate its ability to produce the notes in normal production, which may have identified technical problems earlier. Instead, the creasing issue was not discovered until BEP had produced 1.4 billion notes, including an unknown quantity of defective notes. The problem delayed the issuance of the $100 note by 2 years and was resolved with assistance from the currency quality assurance program (CQA). This program, which is funded by the Federal Reserve, seeks to prevent the types of problems that arose with the $100 note through formal development programs for note design, which include interagency reviews. The development of the tactile feature is one of the pilot projects under the CQA program.

BEP and Federal Reserve Officials Have Discussed Federal Reserve Concerns about the Current Approach

BEP has indicated that the Federal Reserve has raised concerns about its current three-pronged approach to provide access to currency for visually impaired persons. While the three-pronged approach has been approved by the Secretary of the Treasury, who is on record as still pursuing this approach, the court order does not require this or any other specific approach. The Secretary has discretion over how to comply with the court order and could modify the current approach. Senior BEP and Federal Reserve officials stated, however, that Treasury and BEP would need to consult the Department of Justice to determine whether any revised approach would satisfy the requirements of the court order. ACB would also retain the ability to challenge whether a modification continues to comply with the court order.

Senior BEP and Federal Reserve officials told us that they have discussed the Federal Reserve's concerns about the potential cost impact of a tactile feature and whether the extent of technological changes since the 2008 court order could provide alternative options to its current approach; however, they remain committed to providing access through their three-pronged approach. Specifically, senior BEP and Federal Reserve officials told us they have discussed whether high contrast numerals, a currency reader program, and the EyeNote smartphone app—without including a raised tactile feature on currency—could meet the requirements of the 2008 court order. Federal Reserve officials expressed concerns about the potential cost impact of a tactile feature on those who handle large amounts of currency, including banks and ATM manufacturers. They stated that meaningful access should be provided in a way that meets the needs of visually impaired persons while being mindful of cost. However, senior BEP and Federal Reserve officials also stated that they are committed to providing meaningful access to currency, and in June 2014, the BEP Director reiterated that the development of a durable tactile feature is a priority for the agency. Furthermore, senior BEP officials stated that BEP would need to take multiple steps before it could consider altering the current approach. For example, the officials said that BEP would have to fully implement its currency reader device program to understand the efficacy of the program. They also said that BEP would need to collect data on the production requirements and costs of a raised tactile feature. BEP officials clarified that while there was a discussion of the option to provide access to currency without adding a tactile feature, no decision has been made.

Advocates for visually impaired persons have concerns about excluding a tactile feature. Most advocates we spoke with told us that high-contrast numerals, a currency reader, and a smart phone app are beneficial to some, but these efforts are not as important as a tactile feature. According to these advocates, a tactile feature is the most effective method to allow a visually impaired person to denominate currency independently and quickly. In July 2014, one advocacy organization passed a resolution stating that a currency reader device program should not be a replacement for a tactile feature.

CONCLUSION

The visually impaired community is diverse, and there is no single way to ensure access to currency for all visually impaired persons. In recognition of this diversity, BEP developed a three-pronged approach to make currency accessible to visually impaired persons. In particular, BEP has incorporated high-contrast, large numerals on some denominations of notes, and plans to continue incorporating them in future redesigns; it has launched the initial phase of its currency reader program; and it has been developing a tactile feature to be incorporated in the next family of redesigned notes. In addition, BEP has created a free currency reader smartphone app, which is currently available.

While these are positive steps, there is no date set for the introduction of a tactile feature, and it will be at least several years until there is a tactile feature on U.S. currency. Even when a tactile feature is introduced, notes with a tactile feature will co-circulate with notes that do not have a tactile feature. As a result, U.S. currency without a tactile feature will be in circulation for many years. Given this time frame, it is important for the currency reader program to be an effective interim step to provide access to currency for visually impaired persons.

BEP has taken some initial steps to evaluate the effectiveness of the currency reader program, a key component of its three-pronged approach; however, these efforts do not provide BEP with complete information about important parts of the currency reader program such as how well the program provides visually impaired persons with a means to independently denominate currency. Program evaluation is a critical strategy that can allow agencies to understand whether a program is addressing the intended problem, to assess the value or effectiveness of the program, and to make changes to improve the design or management of an existing program. Without a complete evaluation of the program, BEP cannot determine whether the currency reader program is reaching users as intended and providing them with appropriate access to currency. The lack of knowledge means that BEP may not be in the best position to make any necessary adjustments in the deployment of the next 2 phases of a program that will be needed for many years.

RECOMMENDATIONS FOR EXECUTIVE ACTION

To determine the extent to which the currency reader program provides assistance to visually impaired persons while a tactile feature is being developed and integrated into the next currency redesign, we recommend that the Director of the Bureau of Engraving and Printing take the following action:

- Evaluate the currency reader program to include facets such as how well the program provides visually impaired persons with a means to independently denominate currency.

AGENCY COMMENTS

We provided a draft of this report to BEP, the Federal Reserve, and the Secret Service. BEP did not take a position on our recommendation. The Federal Reserve provided written comments, in which it stated that it is important for visually impaired persons to have access to U.S. currency. BEP and the Federal Reserve also provided technical comments, which we incorporated as appropriate.

David Wise Director
Physical Infrastructure Issues

APPENDIX I: OBJECTIVES, SCOPE, AND METHODOLOGY

The objectives of this report are to examine (1) the status of the Bureau of Engraving and Printing's (BEP) efforts to provide currency that is accessible for visually impaired persons and how BEP is considering costs as part of these efforts, and (2) factors that may affect BEP's efforts to make currency accessible for visually impaired persons.

To obtain information on our objectives, we reviewed relevant documentation and written reports as discussed below. We also interviewed officials from federal government entities directly involved in the design and production of U.S. currency. We also spoke with representatives from advocacy organizations representing blind and visually impaired persons, trade associations from industries that would be affected by changes to U.S. currency, and the Bank of Canada as shown in table 2.

Table 2. Organizations We Interviewed

Federal government	Bureau of Engraving and Printing
	Federal Reserve Board of Governors
	United States Secret Service
Advocacy organizations	American Council of the Blind
	National Federation of the Blind
	Blinded Veterans Association
	National Council on Disability
Industry trade associations	American Bankers Association
	Independent Community Bankers of America
	National Automatic Merchandising Association
	ATM Industry Association
Other government	Bank of Canada

Source: GAO analysis. | GAO-14-823.

We selected the stakeholders for each group based on different criteria. We selected four advocacy organizations that had nationally representative membership and were part of BEP's outreach efforts to visually impaired persons. We selected four industry trade associations for companies that handle currency frequently, such as banks and vending machine manufacturers. Specifically, we selected associations with nationally representative membership. We selected the Bank of Canada, which is the central bank for Canada, because it incorporated a tactile feature on its currency and established a currency reader program; BEP officials reached out to Canadian officials specifically about these efforts. The results of the interviews are not generalizable, but do provide insights regarding efforts to make currency accessible to blind and visually impaired persons.

To obtain information on both of our objectives, we reviewed BEP documents related to BEP's efforts to provide currency that is accessible and interviewed officials from the BEP. We reviewed documents related to the 2002 court case and BEP's semi-annual progress reports to the court. We interviewed officials from the Board of Governors of the Federal Reserve System (Federal Reserve), and the United States Secret Service (Secret Service).

To identify and discuss factors that may affect BEP's efforts to make currency accessible for visually impaired persons, we reviewed documents and interviewed officials from BEP and the Federal Reserve. We also interviewed representatives of 4 national advocacy organizations for visually impaired persons and 4 trade associations that represent financial institutions and companies that use cash handling equipment, such as ATM manufacturers. We interviewed Bank of Canada representatives on its efforts to produce currency that is accessible to visually impaired persons and its currency reader device program.

We conducted this performance audit from February 2014 to September 2014 in accordance with generally accepted government auditing standards. Those standards require that we plan and perform the audit to obtain sufficient, appropriate evidence to provide a reasonable basis for our findings and conclusions based on our audit objectives. We believe that the evidence obtained provides a reasonable basis for our findings and conclusions based on our audit objectives.

End Notes

[1] For the purposes of this report, we refer to blind and low vision persons as visually impaired.

[2] For the purposes of this report, currency refers to paper money, also known as Federal Reserve Notes.

[3] National Research Council of the National Academies, Currency Features for Visually Impaired People (Washington, D.C.: 1995). A literature search did not identify a similar but more recent study.

[4] Currency in the form of coins is easier for visually impaired persons to distinguish because of the differences between denominations, such as size, texture, and color.

[5] Specifically, the lawsuit alleged that Treasury violated Section 504 of the Rehabilitation Act of 1973 (29 U.S.C. §794), which prohibits discrimination against people with disabilities in programs or activities receiving federal financial assistance or under any program or activity conducted by an executive agency or the U.S. Postal Service.

[6] The Secretary of the Treasury appealed the ruling to the United States Court of Appeals for the District of Columbia Circuit, which affirmed the district court's ruling and remanded the case for the district court to address the request for injunctive relief. Am. Council of the Blind v. Paulson, 463 F. Supp. 2d 51 (D.D.C 2006), aff'd, Am. Council of the Blind v. Paulson, 525 F. 3d 1256 (D.C. Cir. 2008).

[7] On remand, the district court granted the Council's request for injunctive relief. Am. Council of the Blind v. Paulson, 581 F. Supp.2d 1 (D.D.C. 2008). Pursuant to the terms of the district court's October 3, 2008, order, Treasury is required to provide meaningful access no later than the date when the Secretary next approves a redesign for that denomination.

[8] Because BEP is responsible for designing and manufacturing banknotes, we generally refer to BEP throughout this report even though the court order was directed to the Secretary of the Treasury.

[9] A range of estimates and a range of sources for those estimates exist. The sources cited here include the U.S. Census Bureau; ARINC Engineering Services, Study to Address Options for Enabling the Blind and Visually Impaired Community to Denominate U.S. Currency, (Maryland, 2009); National Council on Disability; and National Eye Institute.

[10] The meanings of terms such as "visually impaired", "blind", and "low vision" can vary depending on their intended use. For example, the Social Security Administration's definition of visual impairment to determine eligibility for disability differs from a state's definition of eligibility for a driver's license.

[11] National Research Council, Currency Features for Visually Impaired People.

[12] In the context of currency, a tactile feature is part of a note that allows a person to determine its value by touch.

[13] The need to address counterfeiting threats is the over-riding reason to make changes to currency. Because the nature of these threats is unpredictable, BEP does not redesign currency on a specific schedule.

[14] The Secretary of the Treasury approved the approach on May 31, 2011.

[15] A currency reader is an electronic assistive device that can identify a note's value and communicate it to the user. BEP originally proposed to loan the readers to eligible participants at no cost. The Comptroller General of the United States issued a decision that BEP could use appropriated funds to purchase and distribute the readers at no cost to the visually impaired as part of its compliance with the district court's order to provide meaningful access to U.S. currency. Matter of: Bureau of Engraving and Printing—Currency Reader Program, B-324588, Comptroller General of the United States, 2013 U.S. Comp. Gen. LEXIS 107, June 7, 2013

[16] 75 Fed. Reg. 28331(May 20, 2010).

[17] In addition to these committees, a fourth, the Technology Approval Committee (TAC) is chartered to make decisions regarding funding, scope, and timelines on technology development projects. In May 2014, the PAC transferred decisions about the tactile feature to the TAC.

[18] By "redesign," we refer to the change in the design of the whole banknote, and not to minor changes BEP occasionally makes, such as to the signature of the Secretary of the Treasury or Treasurer of the United States.

The first redesigned family of notes, known as Series 1996, were issued from 1996–2000. The second family of notes, Series 2004, were issued from 2003–2013.

[19] Examples of statutory requirements include that notes must be printed using a specific type of printing plates, must have "In God We Trust," (31 U.S.C. § 5114) and must have a serial number assigned by the Federal Reserve. 12 U.S.C. § 413.

[20] Consolidated Appropriations Act 2014, Pub. L.No 113-76, §113, 128 Stat 5, 191.The 2008 court order excludes the $1 note.

[21] The inkwell security feature contains a color-shifting bell that changes from copper to green as the note is tilted.

[22] NLS and BEP staff certified applicants' eligibility and provided readers at each conference.

[23] BEP's contract with the supplier requires that the reader successfully denominate notes 98 percent of the time.

[24] GAO, Program Evaluation: Strategies to Facilitate Agencies' Use of Evaluation in Program Management and Policy Making, GAO-13-570 (Washington, D.C.: June 26, 2013). GAO found that 80 percent of federal managers who had recent program evaluations reported that the evaluations contributed to assessing the program's effectiveness or value.

[25] A denominating pattern is a consistent approach used to provide easy identification of each denomination of currency.

[26] Before deciding to include a raised tactile feature as part of its three-pronged approach to make currency accessible, BEP considered and rejected other tactile options for banknotes, including varying the size of each denomination, notching their edges, and punching holes.

[27] Bureau of Engraving and Printing, White Paper Regarding Meaningful Access to U. S. Currency for Blind and Visually Impaired Individuals (Washington, D.C., June 27, 2013).

[28] Pursuant to statute, certain matter mailed for or sent by the blind and other handicapped persons who cannot use or read conventionally printed material may be mailed free of postage. See 39 U.S.C. §§ 3403, 3404, and 3405

[29] In addition to cost, BEP evaluated the durability, usability, and risk of each application method.

[30] One application method costs significantly less than others because BEP could use its existing equipment.

[31] The information on costs is based on preliminary information from the Federal Reserve's Cash Product Office and a 2014 survey of Federal Reserve Banks, banknote equipment manufacturers, depository institutions, and armored carriers.

[32] According to BEP documents, a tactile feature could potentially increase the height of stacked currency. Transportation costs for ATMs could increase because ATMs would hold fewer notes and need to be refilled more frequently.

[33] ARINC Engineering Services, Study to Address Options for Enabling the Blind and Visually Impaired Community to Denominate U.S. Currency (Maryland: 2009).

In: U.S. Currency and the Blind and Visually Impaired   ISBN: 978-1-63463-903-3
Editor: Arlene Truman   © 2015 Nova Science Publishers, Inc.

Chapter 2

WHITE PAPER REGARDING MEANINGFUL ACCESS TO U.S. CURRENCY FOR BLIND AND VISUALLY IMPAIRED INDIVIDUALS[*]

Bureau of Engraving and Printing

EXECUTIVE SUMMARY

The mission of the Bureau of Engraving and Printing (BEP) is to develop and produce U.S. currency (Federal Reserve notes) that is trusted worldwide. As its primary function, the BEP prints approximately 6.5 to 8.5 billion Federal Reserve notes each year depending on an annual order from the Board of Governors of the Federal Reserve System (the Board). As the issuing authority, the Board takes delivery of the Federal Reserve notes from the BEP and issues them to the Federal Reserve Banks which, in turn, distribute them to the public through depository institutions that have a Federal Reserve account.

In June 2012, the Senate Committee on Appropriations issued Senate Report 112-177. This report directed "the BEP to report to Congress and to Treasury's Office of Inspector General (OIG) within 90 days of enactment [the 2013 Financial Services and General Government Appropriations bill] on a detailed plan, including a timeline, to develop, design, test, and print currency with accessibility features. The plan should also include an analysis of the feasibility of expediting the Federal acquisition process for the specialized equipment required to create accessibility features. The Committee directs the OIG to provide an initial assessment of the plan to the Committee within 60 days of receipt and to report on its progress and implementation every 6 months thereafter until the plan is fully implemented." Although the legislation accompanying the Senate Report was not enacted, given the high level of interest, and to enhance communication and openness, the BEP is submitting this white paper to the Treasury OIG and the Senate Committee on Appropriations.

In October 2008, the United States District Court for the District of Columbia issued its ruling in *American Council of the Blind v. Paulson,* holding that the Secretary of the

---

[*] This is an edited, reformatted and augmented version of a report issued by the U.S. Bureau of Engraving and Printing, June 27, 2013.

Department of the Treasury "violated Section 504 of the Rehabilitation Act," and requiring the Secretary to "take such steps as may be required to provide meaningful access to United States currency for blind and other visually impaired persons" in conjunction with the subsequent redesign of each denomination of currency approved by the Secretary.

To take a comprehensive, informed approach, the BEP commissioned a study in 2008 to: (1) review and analyze the needs of the blind and visually impaired community; (2) examine methods available at that time that could potentially improve access to Federal Reserve notes; (3) perform a cost impact analysis of the possible accommodations on various government and industry sectors; and (4) provide a decision model whereby the BEP could compare and contrast various accommodations. The BEP published the final study report on its website when it was received in July 2009.

Results from the study confirmed that there is no single solution that will enable all segments of the blind and visually impaired population to denominate U.S. currency with 100 percent accuracy. As such, the BEP recommended three actions to the Secretary of the Treasury to provide meaningful access, which were approved on May 31, 2011. Those accommodations are:

1. Inclusion of a raised tactile feature to each Federal Reserve note the BEP is permitted by law to alter.[1] This feature would provide users with a means of identifying each denomination via touch;
2. Continuation of the process of adding large, high-contrast numerals and different colors to each denomination that the BEP is permitted by law to alter; and
3. Distribution of currency readers to blind and visually impaired U.S. citizens and those legally residing in the United States that would allow users to denominate U.S. currency.

In addition, since the 2008 order was issued, technology has advanced dramatically.

Accordingly, the BEP has provided immediate accommodation to a segment of the blind and visually impaired population by issuing banknote denominating applications (apps) for mobile devices.

The BEP has made progress implementing the Secretary's approved accommodations. First, the BEP has performed rigorous analyses of several aspects of applied tactile features. The BEP is evaluating material and application methods for ease of application, cost, and tactility, in addition to durability in circulation. The BEP continues to test various patterns and shapes of tactile features to optimize their effectiveness for the blind and visually impaired community.

The BEP anticipates it will have the application method (which determines the equipment type required) selected in December 2013 and the application material selected by January 2015. At this point, the tactile feature will be ready for transfer to the banknote development process, which is the incorporation of features into a design concept that has been purposefully developed to accommodate all the security and functionality requirements for banknotes in the environment in which they will circulate. The banknote development process is designed to end in a secure, producible Federal Reserve note.

As part of the next Federal Reserve note redesign process, in addition to the raised tactile feature, the BEP will continue to include large, high-contrast numerals similar to the $5 note issued in 2008 to help the visually impaired better denominate U.S. currency.

As noted previously, the BEP has already provided currency readers to a segment of the blind and visually impaired population by issuing banknote denominating apps for mobile devices. The larger (not mobile app) currency reader distribution program is planned for a nationwide launch in 2015. The BEP is in the process of procuring currency readers and acquiring additional program resources for administering the program. The BEP is also working with the National Library Service of the Library of Congress (NLS), which provides book readers to the blind and visually impaired, to develop an Inter-Agency Agreement whereby NLS would assist the BEP in distributing currency readers.

Tactile features will be incorporated through the U.S. currency redesign process, the timing and content of which is largely driven by the level and nature of security threats to Federal Reserve notes. At the same time as BEP is developing tactile features, it is working closely with the Board, the United States Secret Service (USSS), and the Departmental Offices of the Treasury (Treasury) to identify threats and determine appropriate measures to respond to them. Redesign often requires seeking out and developing technology for both overt and covert security features, which requires a lengthy technical development process. As with tactile features, security features developed through the technical development process are transferred to the banknote development process for integration into a producible Federal Reserve note. Due to the interrelated nature of the various processes, the overall creation of any one Federal Reserve note design is a lengthy and complex endeavor.

The BEP, therefore, anticipates that the first redesigned denomination containing a tactile feature, an improved large, high-contrast numeral, and new security features to be released for circulation in 2020. The estimated timeline for the complete process is shown in Figure 1.

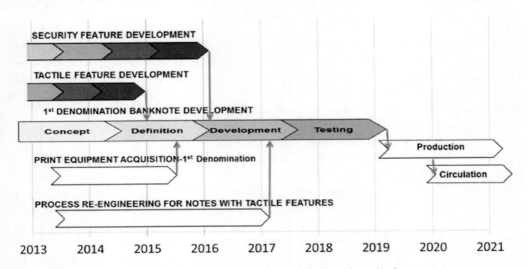

Figure 1. Timeline to commence circulation of first denomination with tactile feature.

At this time, testing for a potential application method is being conducted at contractor sites, before the BEP acquires any additional equipment required to add tactile features to Federal Reserve notes. Any acquisition will only proceed once an application method has been selected. The BEP will do all that it can to accelerate the acquisition of this equipment while complying with the requirements to the Federal Acquisition Regulation. At present, the BEP does not plan to seek a waiver from full and open competition.

The projection of initial circulation of redesigned currency with a tactile feature in 2020 depends on much more than just the successful design and integration of a tactile feature. The release date is also dependent on technology/security feature development, production issues, and other unanticipated developments.

We anticipate that the next redesigned denomination, the first one with the tactile feature, will be the $10 Federal Reserve note. When deliberating the various options for the next denomination to be redesigned, the Advanced Counterfeit Deterrence Steering Committee (ACD)[2] engages in a detailed analysis consisting of a counterfeit threat assessment, the state of security feature development to counter such threats, production capabilities and complexities, societal issues, relative use of various notes in transactional commerce, and impact on consumers and banknote equipment manufacturers. Following its analysis, the ACD recommended the $10 note. The $10 note was also selected because it is a transactional note used frequently in commerce and it has a low production volume, which will allow for the smoothest transition of a new complex design to manufacturing. Once production begins, the Board, as the issuing authority, will determine when the redesigned $10 Federal Reserve note is put into circulation. However, should security threats against another denomination occur, the next denomination to be redesigned could change.

Development of a durable, easy to use tactile feature for the blind and visually impaired is a priority for the BEP, and its most senior personnel have been tasked with this complex endeavor.

BACKGROUND

In May of 2002, the American Council of the Blind, a national advocacy group representing the blind and visually impaired community, and two visually impaired individuals, brought suit against the Secretary of the Treasury alleging that the Department of the Treasury was not providing meaningful access to the currency for blind and other visually impaired individuals, and thus was in violation of Section 504 of the Rehabilitation Act, 29 U.S.C. § 794.

On October 3, 2008, the United States District Court for the District of Columbia (Court) issued its ruling in *American Council of the Blind v. Paulson*, that the Secretary violated Section 504 of the Rehabilitation Act, and required the Secretary to "take such steps as may be required to provide meaningful access to United States currency for blind and other visually impaired persons" in conjunction with the subsequent redesign of each denomination of Federal Reserve notes approved by the Secretary. The Court specifically recognized the complexity of banknote design and ordered that action be taken within the context of the next currency redesign. This is the schedule the BEP is working toward, as the yet uncirculated $100 Federal Reserve note is the final note of the last redesign. The Court also required the BEP to provide a status report every six months. The order does not apply to the $1 Federal Reserve note, which the BEP is prohibited from redesigning, or the redesigned $100 Federal Reserve note that is scheduled to begin circulating in October 2013.

In January 2008, prior to the Court's October 3 ruling, the BEP commissioned a comprehensive study to: 1) review and analyze the needs of the blind and visually impaired community; 2) examine methods available at that time that could potentially improve access to Federal Reserve notes; 3) perform a cost impact analysis of the possible accommodations on various government and industry sectors; and 4) provide a decision model whereby the BEP could compare and contrast various accommodations. The BEP received the results of the study in July of 2009. That report is posted on the BEP website at: http://www.money factory.gov/images/ARINC Final Report 7-26-09.pdf.

The report outlined the cost-benefit analysis for note size variation, tactile features, machine-readable features and currency reader devices. Based upon the study and the BEP's experience in banknote design and manufacturing, the BEP concluded that there is no single solution that will enable all segments of the blind and visually impaired population to denominate Federal Reserve notes with 100 percent accuracy. Therefore, the BEP recommended three strategies to permit those who are blind or visually impaired to denominate U.S. currency accurately and quickly, and which at the time did not appear to place an undue burden on the BEP, the Federal Reserve System, U.S. businesses, or domestic and international users. These recommendations went above and beyond the Court's 2008 Order, and expanded the scope of the BEP's plans to improve access to currency for blind and visually impaired persons. As we move forward, additional societal and government costs will be considered.

The BEP posted its proposed recommendations in the Federal Register in May, 2010, considered approximately 50 public comments submitted in response to that notice, consulted with the Interagency Currency Design Group (ICD)[3], and received concurrence from the Advanced Counterfeit Deterrence Steering Committee (ACD) on the proposed course of action. The BEP recommended the following:

1. Include a raised tactile feature on each Federal Reserve note the BEP is permitted by law to alter. This feature would provide users with a means of identifying each denomination via touch;
2. Continue the practice of adding large, high-contrast numerals and different colors to each denomination that the BEP is permitted by law to alter; and
3. Distribute currency readers to blind and visually impaired U.S. citizens and those legally residing in the United States that would allow users to denominate U.S. currency.

The BEP recommended that the currency reader program be implemented as soon as possible to provide an accommodation to the blind and visually impaired population, while addressing the inevitable period of transition during which Federal Reserve notes with and without tactile features and large, high-contrast numerals will co-circulate. The Secretary of the Treasury approved the proposal on May 31, 2011, pursuant to his authority under 12 U.S.C. § 418 to make final decisions relating to currency design.

To enhance the accessibility of Federal Reserve notes, the BEP considered several options including variable size banknotes, notches, materials embedded in or applied to the surface of the substrate, machine readable materials, and perforations. Based on the information contained in the 2009 study, published information regarding scientific study based on the sense of touch, referred to as "haptic" response, and the effectiveness of tactile features in banknotes around the world, the BEP decided the best method of providing a means to denominate Federal Reserve notes by touch was to develop a raised tactile feature for application to the surface of the banknote. Since approval of this approach, significant progress has been made.

DEVELOPMENT OF THE TACTILE FEATURE

The BEP continues to perform rigorous analyses of several aspects of applied tactile features. For example, the BEP is testing, for durability and producibility, features using special inks and other materials applied to the surface of the substrate, features embedded into the substrate, features that involve alterations to the substrate, and features using intaglio[4] print techniques. The BEP is developing options internally and with outside vendors, and has defined a selection methodology to identify the most durable and effective tactile feature possible.

The location of a tactile feature on a Federal Reserve note appears not to be critical to its interpretation; users can be educated as to the location. There are, however, considerations that make some locations preferable to others. For instance, locating the tactile feature along either the top or bottom (horizontal) edge of the Federal Reserve note allows users to utilize the feature without removing the banknote completely from a wallet or purse. Many who participated in feature reviews expressed this preference.

The BEP has also investigated the design of the tactile feature element, combinations of elements to form a denomination scheme, materials, application methods, materials used to increase adherence, and the position of the feature on the banknote. The BEP chose not to directly adopt tactile features used by other countries given the higher durability requirements for the worldwide circulation of Federal Reserve notes and the extended life of those notes in circulation.

The BEP conducted a usability study in 2011 with a subject matter expert in the field of touch perception to identify the most perceptible and effective tactile feature symbol designs. In addition, over the past two years the BEP has shared various samples containing prototype raised tactile features with members of the blind and visually impaired community at a variety of conferences, conventions, and meetings to get feedback regarding the usability of the different styles of features being investigated. The BEP has developed a protocol for testing the usability of potential features, in concert with experts in such studies and several advocacy organizations.

As a result of this research, the BEP has narrowed down the field of possible features and is now testing these features. It is anticipated that the application method (which determines the equipment type required) will be selected in December 2013 and the application material will be selected by January 2015. Selection of an acceptable material and application method involves evaluation for ease of application, cost, and tactility (governed by several factors), in addition to retention on the substrate, and durability with extended wear. The BEP must ultimately select a combination that is durable, cost-effective to produce, compatible with high-speed manufacturing and processing equipment, and minimally impacts existing cash handling and banknote verification machines.

After considering a large number of options and feedback from the blind and visually-impaired community, the BEP is proceeding with a single symbol design and denominating scheme. Based upon its current research efforts, the BEP has determined a hollow rectangle to be highly perceptible by touch (Figure 2). The notional size for each single rectangle is 6mm (vertical) by 4mm (horizontal).

▯

Figure 2. Most Likely Tactile Feature Shape.

This conclusion was reached after exploring prototype samples that contain different symbol shapes including circles, triangles, ovals, slanted lines, six-dot clusters, and others that were evaluated by members of the blind community. In order to validate the information acquired during these informal sessions with blind users, the BEP contracted a subject matter expert to conduct a formal, scientifically-based acuity study designed to compare the relative ease with which the various symbol shapes could be recognized by touch. The results of this study, conducted in late 2011, clearly validated the results of the information informally collected by the BEP.

To date, the most promising denominating scheme appears to be a 4-position pattern (Figure 3), with a 14mm spacing between adjacent symbols (18mm on center) to enhance the user's ability to distinguish single symbols within the denominating scheme. The user would denominate the note by the number and location of elements in the pattern. This scheme represents a good balance between ease of use and optimization of available space on the surface of a Federal Reserve note. An added advantage to this scheme is its similarity to that used on Canadian banknotes that have been in circulation for many years and have been accepted by blind users.

▯   ▯   ▯   ▯

Figure 3. Likely Denominating Feature for $50 note. The pattern for the $50 was used because it shows the maximum impact on the design and it represents all possible locations of the pattern on the note.

Because of long lead time necessary to address the significant security feature development and process issues discussed below, the BEP estimates that the redesigned $10 Federal Reserve note containing a tactile feature and new security features will be ready for production in 2019. From that point, it is estimated that it will take six to twelve months to print enough Federal Reserve notes to meet Board requirements prior to the banknotes entering circulation in 2020.

DEVELOPMENT OF LARGE, HIGH-CONTRAST NUMERALS

In 1997, the BEP began adding large, high-contrast numerals and different colors to U.S. currency. This was part of the redesign of the Series 1996 $50 Federal Reserve note. In March 2008, the BEP introduced the current $5 Federal Reserve note design, which improved upon the earlier design by increasing the size and contrast of the large numeral. The feedback received from visually impaired individuals regarding their ability to independently denominate Federal Reserve notes by using these numerals has been positive. This feature was continued in the redesigned $100 Federal Reserve note scheduled for release in 2013, and the BEP will continue to refine this feature in future U.S. currency redesigns. Specifically, as part of the Federal Reserve note design process, the BEP will explore a number of options concerning the size, color, placement, background contrast, and other attributes for these large numerals with the aim of improving accessibility of Federal Reserve notes for persons with visual impairments.

DEVELOPMENT OF THE CURRENCY READER PROGRAM

Based on the study completed in 2009, the BEP recommended a currency reader distribution program in which the BEP would provide a currency reader to eligible blind and visually impaired persons at no cost to them. A currency reader is a small hand-held device that identifies the denomination of an individual Federal Reserve note when a user inserts the banknote into the device. The currency reader program aims to provide a means to denominate U.S. currency during the co-circulation of Federal Reserve notes with and without a tactile feature and large, high-contrast numeral. The BEP intends to launch the currency reader distribution program in advance of issuing tactile-enhanced Federal Reserve notes. The BEP expects this currency reader program to be needed for many years because: 1) current law prohibits redesign of the $1 Federal Reserve note; 2) tactile-enhanced Federal Reserve notes are expected to be issued one denomination at a time; and 3) current-design notes without tactile features are expected to co-circulate with tactile-enhanced Federal Reserve notes for many years.

Given these restrictions, the BEP intends to launch a nationwide rollout of the currency reader program in 2015. To that end, the BEP is in the process of procuring currency readers and acquiring additional program resources for administering the program, and expects to award a contract in 2014. The BEP is in discussions with the National Library Service (NLS) of the Library of Congress to obtain its support in administering elements of the currency reader program for the BEP through an Inter-Agency Agreement (IAA). Indeed, the BEP's framework for the currency reader program is inspired by the NLS program to loan library materials and book readers to blind and other disabled persons. The BEP therefore believes that obtaining NLS support will add efficiency to development and implementation of the currency reader program.

To support the IAA, in June 2013, the Government Accountability Office (GAO) issued an opinion that it was acceptable to transfer title (ownership) of currency readers to blind and visually impaired individuals, as opposed to lending readers. This will reduce the burden of administering a loaned reader program and the BEP is moving forward with a program designed around giving currency readers to eligible individuals.

DEVELOPMENT OF TECHNOLOGY-BASED APPLICATIONS

In the Federal Register notice published in 2010, the BEP indicated that in addition to the three recommended approaches, it would continue to explore emerging technological solutions to provide improved access to Federal Reserve notes to the blind and visually impaired. The BEP recognized that the proliferation of mobile phones used by consumers, specifically a growing number of blind and visually impaired individuals, created an additional opportunity to use technology as way to provide meaningful access to currency.

To seize this opportunity, in 2010, the BEP developed the EyeNote® application (app), designed to allow individuals to scan and denominate Federal Reserve notes using a mobile device operating on the Apple iOS platform. The app is available as a free download on the Apple App Store**SE**. The BEP also collaborated with the Department of Education to introduce a similar, free app that operates on Android-based mobile devices; the IDEAL Currency Reader interacts with Google's "Eyes-Free" application and can be downloaded from Google Play. These applications are providing an immediate accommodation for a segment of the blind and visually impaired population, and may result in lower demand for currency readers.

OTHER CONSIDERATIONS

Security Features Development

U.S. currency redesign is primarily done in response to security threats posed by banknote counterfeiting. As the quantity and sophistication of threats to Federal Reserve notes increase, so must the complexity of the security features embodied in future designs. The Treasury, the BEP, the USSS, and the Board work closely together to monitor threats to U.S. currency, and to identify and develop new security features to counter those threats. The ACD makes recommendations to the Secretary of the Treasury on redesigns, directs the development of advanced deterrent technology, and coordinates public education related to the latest designs and features to deter counterfeiting. A typical Federal Reserve note design will include several different levels of security features, each specifically designed to permit detection and rejection of counterfeits by the Federal Reserve System and users of U.S. currency.

The primary strategic goals of redesign are to: 1) include in Federal Reserve notes unique and technologically advanced features to deter counterfeiting; 2) facilitate the public's use and authentication of Federal Reserve notes, and; 3) promote global public confidence in U.S. currency. The development of features or technologies uses a structured approach, referred to as the technology development process. This process, while still under development, is intended to ensure that the requirements of the numerous stakeholders are met, and promote an organized and logical exploration of emerging technologies to "stay ahead" of counterfeiters and constantly-advancing technologies, materials, and processes available to them. This structured approach is depicted in Figure 4.

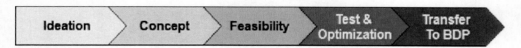

Figure 4. Technology Development Process.

The technology development process utilizes multiple sources for new security technologies, including National Academy of Sciences studies, internal research and development, technical conferences, market sector vendor outreach, industry experts, other Federal agencies, and national laboratories. This formal process, with stage-gate reviews for evaluation of potential security features, is an integral part of the BEP's methodology to achieve its strategic objectives. Each idea is carefully screened and evaluated by an interagency technical group. Promising features are subjected to thorough evaluation of feasibility. Features determined to be feasible are subjected to a rigorous test and optimization process, from prototyping through large scale manufacturing. Ultimately, features selected are transferred into the banknote development process (BDP) where all features and design components are integrated into a producible, highly secure Federal Reserve note. This structured approach is depicted in Figure 5.

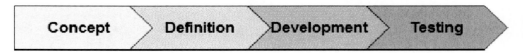

Figure 5. Banknote Development Process.

The newly redesigned $100 Federal Reserve note provides an outstanding illustration of the challenges that can result from inclusion of new security features in a banknote. The new $100 Federal Reserve note includes several new anti-counterfeiting features, including a three-dimensional security ribbon that appears to be "woven" into the substrate, and a feature in which the image of a bell disappears and reappears as its color changes when tilting the banknote. These features, more sophisticated than those previously incorporated into Federal Reserve notes, caused several manufacturing problems that the BEP did not foresee. Specifically, during initial production it was noticed that occasionally a sheet of notes (32 banknotes per sheet) would crease. The BEP, along with the Board, the USSS, and our suppliers have been working to understand the cause of the creasing, and to mitigate the causes of this problem. The BEP is now successfully printing the new $100 Federal Reserve notes and the Board has announced they are scheduled to begin circulating in October 2013.

The Federal government has already begun planning a new family of Federal Reserve note designs. In November 2012, the ACD endorsed a recommendation that the next denomination to be redesigned should be the $10 Federal Reserve note and that, in addition to the tactile feature, it must include new security features that facilitate the goal of staying ahead of emerging counterfeit threats. To prevent the problems that arose with the $100 Federal Reserve note, the BEP has implemented a more sophisticated and rigorous pre-production process, along with continuous quality improvement. This process is part of the Currency Quality Assurance (CQA) program and is aimed at ensuring that future U.S. currency designs meet all of the needs of the BEP's stakeholders, are producible, and are developed as efficiently as possible under a more formal and controlled protocol.

DESIGN OF NEW BANKNOTES

The CQA process is a joint effort between the BEP and the Federal Reserve Board, and has included the services of an external organization with product quality expertise. The CQA process has defined a robust technology and product development process for all Federal Reserve note redesigns.

The technical development process and the banknote development process guide the development of a single Federal Reserve note. For any one denomination, these two processes are expected to take 10 to 12 years, or longer should an adequate number of security features fail to reach maturity. The ACD has adopted a policy of developing Federal Reserve note designs as a family. Banknotes within a family usually have a very similar architecture, but may have different security features depending on the nature of the security threat. Because of this, each Federal Reserve note redesign within a family is undertaken individually, which produces a staggered, denomination-specific development schedule.

PRODUCTION

The final stage of the banknote design process is testing or production validation. During this phase, banknote presses run up to full-production speeds and variations are introduced to determine the sensitivity of the production process. Once the process is understood and optimized, full-rate production can begin. U.S. currency production involves a system of six printing and processing steps. Assuming that the tactile feature application is a separate operation within the larger production process, the time required for a Federal Reserve note to go through the production process would be approximately 35 calendar days.

RE-ENGINEERING THE PRODUCTION PROCESS

Depending on the tactile feature selected, it is likely that the BEP will need to purchase equipment in order to apply the tactile element to the Federal Reserve note substrate. Installation of this equipment will require integration into current production and IT systems and may require facilities renovation. The amount of equipment required for a new design depends upon a number of factors, including the number of Federal Reserve notes of each denomination to be printed.

The complexity of this challenge should not be underestimated; adding a tactile feature will significantly complicate the Federal Reserve note production process. To maximize utility for target users, the tactile features will be located in one position on the note adding thickness to stacks of notes; the added thickness will create feeding, cutting and packaging, as well as inventory issues for Federal Reserve notes, which will likely render current equipment incapable of processing them without costly modifications. Modifications may also be required to the Board's inventory control and accountability systems and its high-speed sorting equipment as well, driven by the increased thickness of banknotes with tactile features. The BEP is currently exploring the impacts of these factors, and will do so in great depth as part of the BDP.

Additionally, the BEP will need to work closely with commercial Banknote Equipment Manufacturers (BEMs), whose cash-handling equipment will be impacted with the addition of tactile features to the Federal Reserve notes. As a general practice, the BEP provides test decks of redesigned banknotes for BEMs to use in upgrading their equipment. The BEP will continue this practice at various stages of development and production of the redesigned $10 Federal Reserve note, to support industry's readiness to recognize and accept the new banknote design.

EQUIPMENT PROCUREMENT

The Federal Acquisition Regulation (FAR) establishes a comprehensive set of procedures that ensures broad, fair competition, a standardized acquisitions process, and lower costs to the government. In addition, the FAR implements the provisions of the Small Business Act, designed to help small/disadvantaged businesses participate in the Federal government's procurement of goods and services. Because the Federal acquisition process can take significant time to complete, adequate time must be included in the acquisition lead-time for proper execution of all required steps.

Acquisition of modified commercially available equipment will certainly require less time than purpose-built equipment. Given the high priority of this task within the BEP, coupled with a plan for direct involvement from senior BEP staff, the process will move in the most efficient manner possible. The BEP will capitalize upon every opportunity to accelerate the acquisition process wherever possible, and thus reduce the time it takes to procure the necessary equipment and materials needed, but does not plan to seek a waiver to the requirements of the FAR for full and open competition.

EQUIPMENT INSTALLATION AND INTEGRATION

Much of the existing processing equipment at the BEP may be capable of processing Federal Reserve notes with tactile features only after modification. Specifically, due to the change in thickness of a banknote with a tactile feature, it is expected that significant modification and/or replacement of machinery may be required in the cutting, stacking, and packaging operations that occur in the latter stages of the banknote production process. Any new or modified equipment must be integrated into the current production process. An analysis to determine the impact of this change is included in the BDP.

The new equipment must also be integrated into the current networked applications designed to manage the high degree of automation and accountability of security paper, ink, and other elements in the production process.

Installation of new machinery also requires extensive modification of facilities to include structural, mechanical, electrical, and plumbing upgrades to support machinery. In addition, the modification must be sequenced carefully to minimize impact to the production schedule. Due to the age of the current buildings at the BEP's Washington, DC facility, the process to prepare a space for installation of new equipment could take up to three years and cost between $3 and $4 million.

OTHER IMPACT

Any new currency design impacts many stakeholders besides the BEP, the Department of the Treasury, and the Federal Reserve System. Many of these stakeholders are likely to incur costs in order to accommodate a Federal Reserve note with tactile features. Devices produced by BEMs may require modification or replacement. Automated Teller Machine (ATM) currency cassettes and handling machinery may require redesign or more frequent replacement to accommodate Federal Reserve notes with tactile features. The vending machine industry may likely experience a similar impact. These costs are likely to be significant.

The tactile feature selected must also be resistant to damage caused by handling machinery and unlikely to damage that same machinery. The BEP, the Department of the Treasury and the Board are aware of these potential impacts, and are working to balance them against the need to field a durable tactile feature that can be readily used by blind and visually impaired persons.

SUMMARY

Development of a durable, easy-to-use tactile feature for the blind and visually impaired is a priority for the BEP, and its most senior personnel have been tasked with this complex endeavor. The BEP has made progress in its Meaningful Access Program. Development of features to provide enhanced access to Federal Reserve notes has been underway at the BEP since 2008. The BEP has been involved in development of both iOS- and Android-based mobile phone applications for denominating currency, which have been available since 2010.

Table 1. Major Milestones in BEP Meaningful Access Program

Intaglio, Coating and Rotary Screen Press Print Trials	Ongoing
Analyze Process Re-engineering and Plant Modifications Requirements	Ongoing
Select Tactile Feature Application Method (Equipment Type)	Dec 2013
Select Tactile Feature Application Material	January 2015
Currency Reader - National Roll-out	2015
Complete Security Feature Development	Early 2016
Complete Process Re-engineering and Plant Modifications (Approximate)	Early 2017
Complete 1st Denomination Banknote Development Process (Approximate)	Early 2019
Commence Production Printing, Banknotes Delivered to Vault (Approximate)	Early 2019
Commence Circulation (Approximate)	Early-Mid 2020

The BEP is now working on the development of an effective tactile feature and is narrowing down the shape, pattern, material, and application method. The BEP expects to have the tactile feature material selected by January 2015, once the appropriate application method has been selected and tested.

The BEP has proven its expertise in developing large, high-contrast numerals and adding different colors to Federal Reserve notes. The BEP will continue to refine these proven denomination methods for future banknote designs.

Significant progress has been made to implement a currency reader program, with the assistance of the Library of Congress, which has experience in distributing free readers to the blind and visually impaired public. We expect the contract for procuring currency readers will be awarded next year, and the process to procure support services for the currency reader program has begun.

The Department of the Treasury and the BEP are committed to implementing the Secretary's recommendations and will continue to work with a sense of urgency. The BEP must balance this urgency with its obligation to provide secure Federal Reserve notes, and to do so following its structured banknote development and production processes. The BEP is confident that it will meet its goal to produce Federal Reserve notes that meet the needs of those who are blind and visually impaired, while maintaining public confidence in U.S. currency.

End Notes

[1] Under current law, the Department of the Treasury is not permitted to redesign the $1 Federal Reserve note. The Consolidated Appropriations Act of 2012, Public Law 112-74, 125 Stat. 786, 890, states that "None of the funds appropriated in this Act or otherwise available to the Department of the Treasury or the Bureau of Engraving and Printing may be used to redesign the $1 Federal Reserve note."

[2] The Advanced Counterfeit Deterrence Steering Committee (ACD) is comprised of senior-level officials from the Department of the Treasury, the Federal Reserve System, and United States Secret Service who coordinate the counterfeit deterrence activities of the government agencies involved in the U.S. currency program.

[3] The purpose of the Interagency Currency Design Group (ICD) is to provide the management infrastructure to support the policies and strategies of the Advanced Counterfeit Deterrence Steering Committee to carry out all the activities necessary to design and produce Federal Reserve notes that meet the security and functional requirements for all users and stakeholders. It consists of senior executives from the Department of the Treasury, the Bureau of Engraving and Printing, the Federal Reserve System, and the United States Secret Service.

[4] Intaglio (in-TAL-ee-oh) is a printing technique in which an image is incised into a surface and the incised lines hold the ink for transfer to the substrate under pressure.

In: U.S. Currency and the Blind and Visually Impaired   ISBN: 978-1-63463-903-3
Editor: Arlene Truman   © 2015 Nova Science Publishers, Inc.

Chapter 3

STUDY TO ADDRESS OPTIONS FOR ENABLING THE BLIND AND VISUALLY IMPAIRED COMMUNITY TO DENOMINATE U.S. CURRENCY[1]

Bureau of Engraving and Printing

ABBREVIATIONS AND ACRONYMS

1-D	one-dimensional sizes
2-D	two-dimensional sizes
ABA	American Bankers Association
ACB	American Council of the Blind
APTA	American Public Transportation Association
ATM	automated teller machine
AU$	Australian dollar
BEP	Bureau of Engraving and Printing
CA$	Canadian dollar
CHF	Swiss franc
CPO	Federal Reserve's Cash Product Office
CTO	Federal Reserve's Currency Technology Office
ECB	European Central Bank
EBU	European Blind Union
EU	European Union
FRB	Federal Reserve Bank
GPS	Global Positioning System
M	millions
NAMA	National Automatic Merchandising Association
NCD	National Council on Disability

---

[1] This is an edited, reformatted and augmented version of a contracted report prepared by ARINC Engineering Services for the U.S. Bureau of Engraving and Printing, dated July 2009. (Note: The appendices mentioned in this report can be found online at http://www.moneyfactory.gov/uscurrency/meaningfulaccess.html under the heading Visual Impairment Study and Appendixes).

NEI	National Eye Institute
NFB	National Federation of the Blind
NHIS	National Health Interview Survey
NRC	National Research Council
OEM	original equipment manufacturer
PIN	personal identification number
ROM	rough order of magnitude
SEK	Swedish kronor
SSA	Social Security Administration
TITO	ticket-in, ticket-out
UK	United Kingdom
U.S.	United States
VI	visually impaired
WHO	World Health Organization

EXECUTIVE SUMMARY

The Bureau of Engraving and Printing (BEP), a bureau within the United States (U.S.) Department of the Treasury, is responsible for designing and producing the U.S. Federal Reserve notes (hereafter referred to as U.S. currency). The BEP initiated this study to examine various aspects of the use of U.S. currency by the blind and visually impaired (VI) population of the U.S. The data, research, and analysis presented in this study will be used to evaluate potential measures that may enhance or improve the ability of the blind and VI to identify currency denominations. Many factors impact the BEP's flexibility in modifying U.S. currency. The BEP must balance printing efficiency, counterfeit deterrence features, statutory requirements, and general banknote aesthetics when it determines a banknote's design to better serve the needs of those who are blind or visually impaired. All of these factors play a vital role in currency design. While this study does not make recommendations, it does provide data regarding future design of U.S. currency that will be useful to the BEP in making such recommendations in the future.

The BEP has engaged ARINC Engineering Services, LLC, an ARINC company, hereafter referred to as ARINC, to conduct a study addressing options for improving the ability of the blind and VI community to denominate[1] U.S. currency. For purposes of this study, ARINC established an "ARINC team" to perform this study through subcontracts with Battelle Memorial Institute, Naois LLC, and the University of Maine. Of note, all ARINC team members are independent from any security paper industry producers and original equipment manufacturers, including hand-held electronic readers, currency raw material or equipment suppliers, or any BEP service providers.

Description of the Study

The ARINC team focused study efforts on currency user requirements and needs of blind and VI people, balanced with the practical and economic implementation considerations of various features. The detailed tasks the ARINC team performed included the following:

- Gathered and analyzed data on the demographic, statistical, and other aspects of the blind and VI population of the U.S.
- Conducted focus group discussions and surveys to assess the needs of the U.S. blind and VI population with respect to identification of U.S. currency denominations.
- Researched currency from countries that have implemented accommodations to meet the needs of the blind and VI to independently denominate currency.
- Conducted one-on-one usability tests to determine how well available accessibility accommodations meet the needs of the blind and VI participants.
- Performed cost and benefit analyses of a group of accommodations (selected by the BEP). The benefit analyses considered the relative effectiveness of the selected accommodations in assisting various segments of the blind and VI population. The cost analyses included operational and technical impacts, and costs to government and industry organizations that manufacture, process, or handle U.S. currency.
- Adapted a decision model to facilitate comparison of currency-related accommodations for the blind and VI. The decision model criteria included provisions for a variety of considerations ranging from functionality of devices to how well the accommodation performs in key usability scenarios for an individual user.
- Customized and updated the decision model to include the cost and subjective aspects of the alternative accommodations.

Number of Blind and Visually Impaired

To determine the number of blind and VI people in the U.S., the ARINC team had to establish a common definition of blindness and visual impairment. The ARINC team found a wide variety of definitions of these terms, as well as a range of different methodologies for estimating the number of affected people. Because of that variation, data on the number of blind and VI people in the U.S. are not consistent. As a result of analyzing the different methodologies and definitions used in previous research, the ARINC team used the following definitions for this study:

- **Blind** = people who have no useful vision for reading any amount of print.
- **Visually Impaired** = people who have difficulty seeing but have some useful vision, defined for this study as being able to read some print (with or without corrective lenses).

Based on available population studies and using the established definitions, the ARINC team estimated that in 2008 there were 304,060 blind people and 4,067,309 VI people in the

U.S. Based on U.S. Government population growth estimates, the ARINC team projects that by 2020, there will be 340,547 blind people and 4,555,386 VI people in the U.S.

Assessment of Needs

To determine the needs of the blind and VI, the ARINC team conducted focus group discussions (Section 3), surveys (Section 4), and usability testing (Section 6). The ARINC team conducted focus groups with blind and VI participants from multiple organizations and demographic groups. Open forum sessions were held at the National Federation of the Blind (NFB) and American Council of the Blind (ACB) 2008 Annual Conventions. There were 402 blind and VI participants in the survey; 249 individuals participated in the focus groups and usability tests.

Through the survey data and focus group discussions, the ARINC team uncovered a number of key currency usage scenarios that blind and VI people find problematic. These scenarios provided a framework for looking at the individual accommodations to see how well they might meet the needs of the blind and VI population. The three problematic scenarios most commonly identified by the study participants were: transactions with no other people in close proximity (such as in a taxi or at a small kiosk), transactions while in a line (people waiting), and conducting a quick inventory of wallet or purse.

Survey results indicate that 72% of all participants said that they would feel less vulnerable if currency were easier for them to use, 72% of all participants felt rushed during transactions, and 70% felt vulnerable using cash. Survey results also indicated that 62% of all participants gave someone incorrect denominations in a transaction in the past year, 60% indicated they would use currency more often if it was easier for them to use, 59% relied on someone at the point of sale to tell them what denominations they were receiving, and 36% of all participants received incorrect change in the past year (e.g., realized after they got home, or not until the next time they used their currency).

Needs of Blind and Visually Impaired Participants

Usability testing and the survey data results confirm that most blind participants in this study desire a way to independently denominate U.S. currency. VI participants in the usability tests were able to correctly denominate most U.S. currency, with over 95% accuracy. VI participants in the usability tests and focus groups said that they preferred accommodations that would enable identification from an arm's length away. For purposes of this study, the ARINC team defined arm's length as approximately one meter. This was based on the National Research Council (NRC) report published in 1995, which noted that a reasonable distance was "approximately one meter, which is roughly the distance from the eye to the checkout counter of a grocery store, enabling easy and rapid identification." [2] More than half (56%) of VI survey participants said they could detect the large purple numeral 5 easier on the newer $5 notes than the smaller green numeral on the older design, but only 17% of them could identify that note at an arm's length distance. Based on the results of both the usability testing and surveys, the ARINC team concluded that the primary desire of the blind and VI is to have the ability to conduct transactions quickly and accurately without causing delay to others waiting in a line.

Analysis of Potential Accommodations

In order to understand the practical implementation issues, the ARINC team conducted (1) international benchmarking activities with countries that have implemented accommodations for blind and VI people, (2) discussions with subject matter experts and scientists (e.g., tactile perception science and color vision impairment), and (3) discussions with individuals in manufacturing and commerce who would produce and handle modified notes. All of these sources helped identify the potential impacts of implementing new accommodations. The results of these investigations, described in Section 5 of this report, were used to plan usability tests and to establish economic analysis parameters.

Several foreign currencies with blind and VI accommodations, four sample currency features, three commercially available currency reader devices, and three prototype currency reader devices were included in the hands-on usability testing portions of the study. Each usability test was recorded via digital video to facilitate collection of speed and accuracy results for each accommodation. Blind and VI participants evaluated a range of accommodations, including changes to color, contrast, and visual design of notes; tactile features; notes of differing sizes for each denomination; and currency reader devices.

Key Findings for Color, Contrast, and Design from Usability Test Results

Color, contrast, and note design features focus on improving note recognition by the VI population in an arm's length transaction scenario. The VI participants in the usability tests demonstrated that high foreground/background contrast for the primary numeral saves them time because they did not have to search both sides of the note for a numeral. VI people in the study who said they had reduced color sensitivity noted that high contrast numbers (e.g., Canadian dollar) were most helpful in aiding them.

Focus group participants indicated that having medium- or large-size numbers in the upper corners, such as used on the United Kingdom (UK) pound, helped them successfully take a quick inventory of note denominations in a wallet.

Extreme differences in the location of features on notes across denominations (e.g., Swedish kronor) allowed VI participants to identify features from further away (up to arm's length) than with currencies that have design items in the same location for all denominations.

Key Findings for Note Size Variation

Feedback from focus groups and survey results indicated that both blind and VI participants believed that they would benefit from note size variation as a way to identify currency denominations. Fifty-two percent of all of the survey participants indicated that size differences would help them denominate currency. Blind participants in the focus groups were very receptive to the concept of size differences as a denomination method. For VI focus group participants, note size variation was considered to be a secondary denomination method to augment visible features.

Results of the usability testing, however, where participants examined a single note at a time without other notes for comparison, indicated that the different sized notes were neither the fastest nor the most accurate method to denominate currency.

Size changes along two dimensions (length and width) resulted in higher average accuracy results in the usability test than changes in only the length dimension. Results for the UK pound (two-dimensional size variation) averaged 60% accuracy, versus average of 48% for the Australian dollar (one-dimensional size variation).

Proportional formats (having incremental increases in length and width) were moderately successful, but did not yield consistently good results. Irregular, or hybrid, size formats (e.g., the Swedish kronor) provided larger differences in length and width. These formats yielded better usability results as measured by accuracy and time to denominate.

It is feasible that more practice and familiarity with a particular accommodation such as sizes could improve the usability of different sized notes.

Key Findings for Tactile Features

Three primary tactile features were included in the usability test. The tested tactile features included a cluster pattern of raised dots, a system of notches cut into the top and bottom edges of the note, and a system of heavy intaglio raised print bars along the side of the note.

Usability test results showed that the prototype edge notches were the most accurate means of identifying denomination for blind participants (average of 89% accuracy). The raised dot clusters, as implemented in Canadian currency, yielded positive results when the currency was essentially new (average of 84% accuracy) but the results for raised dots were significantly degraded on widely circulated notes (average of 49% accuracy). The prototype intaglio print raised bars were very helpful when new (average of 85%), but had similar results as the raised dots when simulated to be well circulated (average of 42%). Usability tests for the other tactile features yielded average accuracy measurements below 75%.

Blind participants had a strong preference for the notches feature, though there was some concern about potential degradation of performance with widely circulated notes. Blind participants said that they used the raised intaglio print numerals on Canadian notes as backup for identification when the raised dots were too worn down to identify.

Fifty-three percent of the survey participants said they thought a tactile feature would help them denominate currency. In the survey results, 43% of all respondents favored multiple accommodations (e.g., combination of a size format and a tactile feature) so that one feature could be used if the other was not discernable.

Key Findings for Currency Reader Devices

Three commercially available currency reader devices were evaluated in usability tests: two devices that require the user to slide the note into a slot in the device, and a cell phone camera- based device. In addition, three developmental prototypes were evaluated: two devices that require the user to slide the note into a slot in the device and a cell phone camera-based device. The ARINC team conducted the usability testing between June 2008 and April 2009, using devices that were operational and available at the time. The ARINC team is aware that technical breakthroughs in this marketplace are occurring at a rapid rate, and the manufacturers of the prototypes tested may make changes to the devices before they become commercially available. Devices currently under development may yield different results than the devices used in this study.

Survey participants were asked if they would take a reader with them when they went out in public. The results were not conclusive—36% of all participants said they would, either occasionally or frequently, 23% said rarely, while 41% said never.

The type of device annunciation (e.g., tone, voice, vibration) is an important consideration for blind and VI people. Most participants preferred voice annunciation when using a device at home, but were concerned about the reader revealing the value of the currency to nearby customers. Usability test participants commented that portability and speed of use are important factors in their willingness to use a reader device. One of the prototype devices received high marks for portability, several participants said they would carry something with similar size and speed with them and would use it while standing in line. Timing is critical in this scenario and most blind participants felt that the commercial devices were too slow for validating notes received as change in a transaction.

Slide-in devices varied in ease of use. Proper use of these devices—orienting the note, sliding it in without folded corners, pressing a button and waiting for response—required varying amounts of dexterity. One of the larger devices was the easiest to use for virtually all participants. The smallest device was easy to use for most participants, and was praised for its portability, but was more challenging for those who had dexterity impairments.

Participants described the need to orient notes for some devices as inconvenient because orienting the note added to the time it took to denominate the currency. Cell phone-based solutions were fairly easy for most participants to use, but took longer to identify the denomination. Participants considered the high cost of currently available devices to be a barrier to implementation.

Economic Analyses of Accommodations

The ARINC team conducted economic analysis of the costs and benefits of seven selected alternative accommodations for blind and VI communities, including: size changes along one dimension, size changes along two dimensions, mechanical tactile features, raised tactile features, embedded tactile features, overt machine-readable features, and currency reader devices. Cost analysis results include initial nonrecurring (one-time) and annual recurring costs associated with each accommodation. The ARINC team considered three top-level categories of costs in this study—U.S. Government (i.e., the BEP, the Federal Reserve Board (FRB), and the U.S. Secret Service), U.S. Market Sectors (i.e., commercial banking, automated teller machines (ATMs), vending, transportation, gaming, and retail equipment), and U.S. Individuals (e.g., the acquisition costs of reader devices).

Cost and Benefit Findings for Note Size Variation

The ARINC team evaluated two size variation approaches, one-dimensional (1-D), where only length varied by denomination and two-dimensional (2-D), where both length and width varied by denomination.

The identified Government and industry costs (including initial nonrecurring investment and annual recurring cost) for implementing size variation accommodations were relatively high— more than $9.5 billion for the first year of 1-D accommodations and more than $10.6 billion for the first year of 2-D accommodations. Blind participants were able to achieve only moderate denomination accuracy (average ranged between 41% and 73%) in usability tests of currency and prototypes with size change accommodations. Distinct two-dimensional note size differences resulted in the highest average speed performance (7.2 seconds) and accuracy (73%) for blind usability test participants for all of the currencies and the prototype with 2-D size differences.

Cost and Benefit Findings for Tactile Features

The ARINC team evaluated three types of tactile features, mechanical (notches along the edges of the notes), raised (raised dots and printed bars), and embedded (foil patches).

Mechanical. The identified Government and industry costs (including initial nonrecurring investment and annual recurring cost) for mechanical tactile features were moderately high— more than $6.6 billion. Blind participants were better at denominating currency using notches than size variation features. Most blind participants were able to denominate the system of notches accurately (average of 89%) and quickly (average of 14 seconds in initial trials, improving to 8.5 seconds with practice).

Raised. The identified Government and industry costs (including initial nonrecurring investment and annual recurring cost) for raised tactile features were moderately high—more than $6.6 billion. Usability testing of raised dots and intaglio printed bars showed the benefits of raised tactile features on new notes. Blind participants were able to use the tactile feature to denominate new Canadian notes accurately (average of 84%). Intaglio printed bars yielded similar results on new notes (average of 85%). However, recognition accuracy for widely circulated notes was significantly reduced for both the raised dots and the intaglio printed bars.

Embedded. The identified Government and industry costs (including initial nonrecurring investment and annual recurring cost) for embedded tactile features were relatively low— more than $568 million. However, embedded tactile features are of limited benefit because they are typically difficult for blind people to locate. Enhancements to existing embedded features would be required to make embedded features a viable option for currency denomination.

Cost and Benefit Findings for Machine-Readable Features

The identified Government and industry costs (including initial nonrecurring investment and annual recurring cost) for machine-readable features were relatively low—more than $75.8 million. There are no direct benefits to the blind and VI population from machine-readable features, unless devices are specifically developed to work with them, but new machine-readable features could enable manufacturers to develop currency reader device technologies that the blind and VI community would be more inclined to use.

Cost and Benefit Findings for Currency Reader Devices

The ARINC team performed a cost analysis and a qualitative benefit analysis of six reader devices (three commercial and three prototype devices) to assess their efficacy as an accommodation for currency denomination by blind people. For the prototype devices, the manufacturers provided an estimated cost, but emphasized that the final price would change based on design changes or estimated market size.

Slide-in note readers provided the greatest benefit among the tested devices. These devices were easiest to learn to use and were very accurate (98% to 99% average accuracy) in relatively short times (average results for individual devices ranged from 17.3 to 21.7 seconds). The estimated purchase price of these devices ranged from $100 to $330.

The commercial cell phone reader device, although highly accurate (average 100%), provided moderate benefit to blind test participants; the denomination time (average of 34.2 seconds) was slower than they preferred. The estimated purchase price of the device was $1,600, but this device provides other applications in addition to currency identification.

The prototype note corner reader was of marginal benefit to the blind test participants because the device accuracy (average 81%) was lower and the denomination speed (average of 36.5 seconds) was slower than the other devices tested. The estimated purchase price of the device was $100.

The prototype cell phone device was too difficult for the blind test participants to use to be beneficial. The estimated price of $30 covers only the software; a cell phone would need to be purchased separately.

1. INTRODUCTION

1.1. Background

The Department of the Treasury's Bureau of Engraving and Printing (BEP) continually seeks input on measures to assist blind and visually impaired (VI) people to more-readily identify United States (U.S.) currency denominations. This has included BEP-sponsored technical and policy studies, including a National Research Council (NRC) report published in 1995.[3] As a result of these technical studies, the BEP included features in recent banknote designs to help VI people denominate U.S. currency. The NRC study made extensive use of published literature and the personal expertise of the study committee members in developing recommendations. However, the NRC study included only limited input from blind and VI individuals and did not evaluate the potential economic impact of the recommendations. The study committee recommended that any future implementation strategy should consider (1) blind and VI community input, (2) economic impact, and (3) the potential for future technical developments that could occur.

The BEP initiated this study to provide the technical information required to enable the BEP to evaluate and implement more effective currency accommodations for blind and VI people.

1.2. Scope

The purpose of this study was to identify and characterize options to improve the ability of blind and VI people to independently denominate U.S. currency. The BEP commissioned this study to identify the needs and issues facing blind and VI people in daily use of U.S. currency, the benefits to be gained from the implementation of various banknote features and accommodations, the technical complexity and life-cycle costs of implementing features and accommodations, and decision model techniques that consider both the benefits to blind and VI users and the costs and technical complexity of implementation.

ARINC assembled a team of experts to complete this study. The team consisted of ARINC (overall program management, economic analyses, cost analyses, logistics support analyses, identification of technological solutions, risk assessment, and impact analyses); Battelle (anti- counterfeiting, security paper manufacturing, and international benchmarking); Naois Corporation (demographics, accessibility needs of blind and VI people, and decision model criteria); and the University of Maine Pulp and Paper Process Development Center (paper manufacturing, paper product development, and quality control). ARINC team members are independent from any security paper industry producers and original equipment manufacturers (including hand-held electronic readers, currency raw material or equipment suppliers, and BEP service providers).

1.3. Currency Accommodations Included in this Study

A 2007 review published by the Federal Reserve Bank of St. Louis[4] summarizes currency design features that have been implemented worldwide to assist blind and VI people with currency denomination. The currency features fall into five major categories:

- Numeral size changes
- Color changes, including primary note colors that differ by denomination as well as printed features, such as numerals with sharp contrast against the background
- Machine-readable features that work with reader devices
- Tactile features, including raised profile features, notched corners and perforations
- Note size changes, varying by denomination

Note size changes and tactile features are designed to aid both blind and VI people, while color changes and numeral size changes are useful principally for VI people. Machine-readable features can facilitate development of devices to identify denominations. This study analyzes these categories of features for both blind and VI people, as appropriate.

In addition to currency features, the ARINC team also evaluated the usability of six candidate reader devices. The ARINC team conducted usability testing between June 2008 and April 2009, using devices that were operational at the time and recognizing that technical breakthroughs in consumer electronics are happening at a rapid rate. Any newly-developed devices entering the market or conceptual design after this time period could be more compact, use different technologies, and could have different results than the devices evaluated in this study.

1.4. Study Technical Approach

The ARINC team focused study efforts on currency user requirements and needs of blind and VI people, balanced with the practical and economic implementation considerations of various features. To accomplish this, the ARINC team performed the following efforts:

- Gathered and analyzed data on the demographic, statistical, and other aspects of the blind and VI population of the U.S.
- Conducted focus group discussions and surveys to assess the needs of the U.S. blind and VI population with respect to identification of U.S. currency denomination.
- Researched data from countries that have implemented accommodations to meet the needs of the blind and VI to independently denominate currency. These accommodations include tactile features, banknotes of different sizes, and currency reader devices. The ARINC team interviewed representatives from international organizations such as the European Central Bank (ECB), the Bank of Canada, and the Canadian Banknote Company; and advocacy groups for the blind and VI such as the National Council on Disability (NCD), the American Council of the Blind (ACB), and the National Federation of the Blind (NFB) to take advantage of lessons learned from previous efforts.
- Conducted usability tests to determine how well currently available accessibility accommodations meet the needs of blind and VI participants.
- Performed cost and benefit analyses of a group of accommodations selected by the BEP. These analyses considered the relative benefits of each of the selected accommodations in assisting various segments of the blind and VI population, as well as the costs to U.S. Government organizations and industry market sectors. The costs and benefits of the accommodations include operational and technical impacts, and cost to businesses, vendors, banks, and other handlers of currency.
- Adapted a decision model to facilitate comparison of currency-related accommodations for the blind and VI. The decision model criteria include provisions for a variety of considerations ranging from an accommodation's compatibility with current security features to the convenience of the accommodation for an individual user.

- Utilized the decision model tool to compare the cost and non-cost aspects of the alternative accommodations.

This report provides an analysis of the blind and VI population of the U.S. (Section 2); the highlights of focus group discussions and surveys (Section 3 and 4, respectively); an analysis of technical considerations and experience for implementation of accommodations for blind and VI people (Section 5); the results of usability testing (Section 6); overview of the economic analysis (Section 7), detailed analyses for each accommodation (Section 8); a summary of the study conclusions (Section 9); and a description of the framework for the decision model to compare the accommodations (Section 10). Detailed data summaries are included in the Appendixes. (Note: Appendixes mentioned in this report can be found online at http://www.moneyfactory.gov/uscurrency/meaningfulaccess.html under the heading Visual Impairment Study and Appendixes)

2. BLIND AND VI COMMUNITIES

2.1. Definitions

There is a wide range of definitions of blindness and visual impairment, as well as a variety of different methodologies for estimating the number of people who are affected by blindness or visual impairment. Because of these variations, data on the number of blind and VI people in the U.S. are inconsistent.

Published statistics on the prevalence of vision impairment are of limited usefulness, primarily because the statistics depend on different definitions of impairment. The U.S. Census Bureau[5] described moderate vision disability as "difficulty seeing small print in a newspaper even when wearing glasses if they normally wear them," and severe vision disability as "unable to see small print in a newspaper."

Lighthouse International summarized a National Health Interview Survey (NHIS) conducted by the National Center for Health Statistics[6] that measured vision loss as "blindness in one or both eyes, or any other reported trouble seeing."

The World Health Organization (WHO) [7] defined blindness (measured in meters) as best corrected visual acuity < 3/60 in the better eye, and low vision as best corrected visual acuity < 6/18 and ≥ 3/60 in the better eye. Using U.S. measurement standards (measured in feet), 6/18 is roughly equivalent to 20/70, and 3/60 is roughly equivalent to 20/400.

The Social Security Administration (SSA)[8] considers blindness as vision that cannot be corrected to better than 20/200 in the better eye, or if the visual field is 20 degrees or less, even with a corrective lens. They state that "many people who meet the legal definition of blindness still have some sight, and may be able to read large print."

Because an objective of this study is to identify people who find it difficult or impossible to denominate currency visually, the ARINC team used the definitions below for this study.

- **Blind** = people who have no useful vision for reading any amount of print.
- **Visually Impaired** = people who have difficulty seeing but have some useful vision, defined for this study as being able to read some print (with or without corrective lenses).

2.2. Published Demographic Data

Assessing the number of blind and VI Americans required evaluation of several data sources. No one source of information was found to be sufficient. However, an approximate number of affected Americans was found using data from NHIS, the Eye Disease Prevalence Research Group, and the National Eye Institute (NEI). Available data required affected population estimates to be derived for two separate age groups (age 40 and below, and over age 40) and then summed to provide a total population assessment. Table 2-1 provides the approximate 2008 U.S. population that is blind and VI.

How these population estimates were derived is described in the following paragraphs. Also, because available population studies use different definitions of vision impairment, Table 2-1 reflects the results of applying factors from the various sources to align these definitions.

A low vision research professional[9], who as a Professor of Ophthalmology has worked in prevalence and incidence of vision impairment, described the information sources used in the following estimates as reliable, but emphasized the difficulty in making accurate estimates based on self-reported vision impairment levels.

2.2.1. Affected Population Size Over Age 40

The Eye Disease Prevalence Research Group estimated that in 2008, 3,638,186 people over age 40 have vision impairment (defined by Eye Disease Prevalence Research Group as having "20/40 or worse vision in the better eye even with eyeglasses") *to include blindness.* They also estimate that of those people 1,035,100 are legally blind; however, they do not provide the criteria used. Subtracting these two numbers yields an estimated 2,603,086 Americans *over age 40,* who have vision impairments.[10] The ARINC team found this study to be the most comprehensive available (albeit only for people over age 40), as it combines results from multiple population surveys that measure visual acuity and reports the number of people affected by visual problems in both eyes. For this study, these numbers need to be adjusted to account for the legally blind people that have some useful vision.

Table 2-1. Blind and VI Population Estimates in 2008

Age Group	Blind	VI
40 and Below	97,040	636,143
Over 40	207,020	3,431,166
Total	304,060	4,067,309

The ARINC team used National Eye Institute (NEI) data[11] to adjust the estimates for the differences in definitions between the Eye Disease Prevalence Research Group estimates and the definitions of blind and VI established for this study. According to NEI estimates, approximately 80% of legally blind people in the U.S. have "some useful vision"; the other 20% have no more than light perception or no vision at all. For purposes of this study, the ARINC team used the NEI estimate of 20%; with the estimated 1,035,100 from Eye Disease Prevalence Research Group to estimate that approximately 207,020 people over age 40 are blind, according to the definition established for this study.

Multiplying the NEI 80% of legally blind that are VI, by the 1,035,100 from Eye Disease Prevalence Research Group, yields 828,080 VI people. Adding this to the 2,603,086 people over age 40 who have vision impairments per the Eye Disease Prevalence Research Group, yields approximately 3,431,166 people over age 40 who are VI, according to the definition established for this study.

2.2.2. Blind Population Size Age 40 and Below

Because data for blind and VI people *at or below age 40* is less well-defined, the ARINC team used a range of available sources to estimate the blind and VI population in this age group. For the purposes of this study, the ARINC team used data from the NHIS National Center for Health Statistics, which estimated that in 1994 there were approximately 1,300,000 legally blind Americans[12]. In July of 1994 the population of the U.S. was approximately 260,402,000[13] (the July 1994 population estimate was derived by using half the difference between U.S. Census Bureau January 1994 and January 1995 estimates). Dividing the approximately 1,300,000 legally blind, as reported by the NHIS National Center for Health Statistics, by the estimated 1994 U.S. population, returns a result of 0.00499 (or 0.5%). This means that in 1994 approximately 0.5% of the entire U.S. population was legally blind. For this study we are using the U.S. Census estimated U.S. population in 2008 of approximately 304,059,724[14] multiplied by the NHIS 0.5% to obtain an estimated legally blind population in 2008 of 1,520,299.

Table 2-2. Blind Population Estimate, Over Age 40 in 2008

Data Source	Blind Over Age 40
Eye Disease Prevalence Research Group	1,035,100
National Eye Institute Adjustment: 20% of legally blind are blind using study definition	1,035,100 * 0.20 = 207,020

Table 2-3. VI Population Estimate, Over Age 40 in 2008

Data Source	VI Over Age 40
Eye Disease Prevalence Research Group	2,603,086
National Eye Institute Adjustment: additional 80% of legally blind are VI using study definition	1,035,100 * 0.80 = 828,080
Total VI Over Age 40	2,603,086 + 828,080 = 3,431,166

Table 2-4. Blind Population Estimate, Age 40 and Below in 2008

Data Source	Blind Age 40 and Below
Legally blind (all ages) 2008 (NHIS 0.5% factor and U.S. Census 2008 estimate)	1,520,299
Blind adjustment (National Eye Institute) 20% of legally blind have no useful vision	1,520,299 * 0.20 = 304,060
Table 2-2 blind over age 40	207,020
Estimated blind age 40 and below	304,060- 207,020 = 97,040

Using available data from NEI, NHIS Center for Health Statistics, and the U.S. Census Bureau, as described above, the following methodology was developed to determine the number of blind people age 40 and below:

A1 = NEI factor that 20% of legally blind are blind using study definition
B1 = 1,520,299 legally blind (all ages) (NHIS 0.5% factor and U.S. Census 2008
    estimate)
C1 = Blind people (all ages, study definition) = A1 x B1 = 304,060
D1 = 207,020 blind people over the age of 40 (Table 2-2)
    Estimated number of blind people age 40 and under = C1 – D1
    = 304,060 – 207,020 = 97,040

2.2.3. VI Population Size Age 40 and Below

A joint report by Prevent Blindness America and NEI titled 'Vision Problems in the U. S. Prevalence of Adult Vision Impairment and Age-Related Eye Disease in America[15] contains charts from which prevalence rates for those VI between the age of 40 and 65 can be estimated. From the vision impairment chart, a prevalence rate of 0.75% was derived by estimating the values of the points for the four age groups shown between 40 years of age and 65 years of age. The four representative values are 0.0005, 0.001, 0.002, and 0.004. These values add up to 0.0075, or 0.75%.

The U.S. Census Bureau estimated that in July 2008 there were approximately 99,565,595 people[16] between the ages of 40 and 65. Using the 0.75% VI factor from above with the estimated 99,565,595 population yields an estimated 746,742 VI people between age 40 and 65.

The NEI Report of the Visual Impairment and Its Rehabilitation Panel [17] report noted that two- thirds (66%) of the total U.S. VI population is over the age of 65. This factor is used with the estimated number of VI people over age 65 to derive the estimate of the total VI population (all ages) as shown below.

A2 = U.S. Census Bureau estimate of 99,565,595[18] people between the ages of 40 and 65
B2 = 0.75% VI prevalence rate (NEI report estimate for between ages 40 and 65)
C2 = 3,431,166 VI over age 40 (Table 2-3)
    D2 = Estimated number of VI over 65 = C2 - (A2 x B2) = 3,431,166 – 746,742 =
    2,684,424

E2 = 66% based on the NEI Report of the Visual Impairment and Its Rehabilitation Panel,[19] estimated that two-thirds (66%) of the total U.S. VI population is over the age of 65

F2 = Estimate of total VI population (all ages) = D2 / E2 = 2,684,424 / 66% = 4,067,309 Estimated total number of VI under the age of 40 = F2 − C2 = 4,067,309 − 3,431,166 = 636,143

2.3. Blind and VI Population Projection

The U.S. Census Bureau[20] estimated a total population of 341,386,665 for 2020, a growth rate of approximately 12% overall from the estimated 2008 population of 304,059,724. The ARINC team used the same relative blind and VI proportions for the U.S. population shown in Table 2-1, with this 12% rate of increase, to project estimated blind and VI population sizes in 2020. Table 2-6 summarizes these projections.

Because the ARINC team cannot predict influencing factors (e.g., environmental factors, medical breakthroughs for improvement, effects of disease) that would impact the rate of blindness or VI, to project values for 2020 the ARINC team used the same relative blind and VI proportions for the U.S. population shown in Table 2-1, with this 12% rate of increase.

2.4. Conclusions – Demographics

The ARINC team used the following definitions for this study:

- **Blind** = people who have no useful vision for reading any amount of print.
- **Visually Impaired** = people who have difficulty seeing but have some useful vision, defined for this study as being able to read some print (with or without corrective lenses).

Table 2-5. VI Population Estimate, Age 40 and Below in 2008

Data Source	VI Age 40 and Below
U.S. Census: people between age 40 and 65	99,565,595
VI adjustment using NEI report prevalence of VI between age 40 and 65: 0.75%	99,565,595 × 0.0075 = 746,742
Table 2-3 VI over age 40	3,431,166
Estimated VI over age 65 (VI over age 40 minus VI between age 40 and 65)	3,431,166 - 746,742 = 2,684,424
Estimate total VI all ages by dividing estimated VI over 65 by VI adjustment of 66% (NEI report estimate that two-thirds of all VI are over age 65)	2,684,424 / 66% = 4,067,309
Estimated VI under 40 = total VI all ages minus VI over 40 (from table 2-3)	4,067,309 − 3,431,166 = 636,143

Table 2-6. Estimated Blind and VI Population Projection for 2020

Age Group	Blind	VI
40 and Below	108,685	712,480
Over 40	231,862	3,842,906
Total	**340,547**	**4,555,386**

Based on available population studies and using the established definitions, the ARINC team estimated that in 2008 there were 304,060 blind people and 4,067,309 VI people in the U.S. Based on U.S. Government population growth estimates, the ARINC team projects that by 2020, there will be 340,547 blind people and 4,555,386 VI people in the U.S.

3. FOCUS GROUPS

The ARINC team conducted focus group sessions, which included open forum discussions and small group sessions, to gather information directly from a broad range of blind and VI participants about their experience with the use of U.S. currency. The basis of the focus group discussions included scenarios for using U.S. currency, challenges using U.S. currency, and common adaptations.

The ARINC team conducted the open forum discussions at the 2008 ACB and NFB Annual Conventions.[21] In addition to these open forum discussions, the ARINC team conducted structured small group interviews that covered a set of core topics (see Focus Group Questions in Appendix A). The small groups included participants from a range of demographic groups— gender, age (children, adults, seniors, or elderly), geographical regions, and vision impairment levels (blind or VI). BEP representatives were present during the open forum discussions to answer questions and participate in informal exchanges of information about BEP operations.

Because of the open format of the focus group discussions, the ARINC team did not record the exact number of people that agreed with each comment. However, the ARINC team used the results of all of the focus group discussions to guide the development of the user experience survey questions (Section 4).

The focus group questions are provided in Appendix A and a summary of participant comments are included in Appendix B. The highlights of the discussions are summarized in Section 3.2. These highlights were taken directly from the focus group participants and represent their stated opinions and experiences.

3.1. Focus Group Participants

Over one hundred blind and VI people participated in the focus groups, creating a broad range of demographics. The ARINC team included the following representative organizations in the focus groups to provide input from a range of participants:

- **Blind and VI veterans:** members of the Washington, DC and Virginia chapters of the Blinded Veterans Association.
- **Blind and VI seniors/elderly:** multiple groups of blind and VI seniors, including seniors (age 65-79) and elderly (age 80 and up) living in independent and assisted-living communities.
- **Blind and VI adults:** (age 18–64) members of the ACB and the NFB from the 2008 annual conventions.
- **Blind and VI children:** minors (age 5–17) at ACB and NFB conventions, as well as at the Perkins School for the Blind.

Table 3-1 provides a summary of participants, by age and vision impairment.

The ARINC team did not assess the statistical significance of the focus group participants because the purpose of the focus groups was to collect qualitative information to use in the development of the survey questionnaire. As discussed in Section 4, the quantitative survey results were analyzed for statistical significance with respect to the blind and VI communities.

3.2. Focus Group Results

3.2.1. Usage Scenarios

Focus group participants described difficulties encountered when using U.S. currency in various scenarios. The scenarios that were discussed are listed below, including key parameters of the situation (e.g., lighting, risk of deception, whether the transaction can be observed, and social pressure to complete the transaction quickly).

- **Transactions with no other people in close proximity, and receiving change**.
  This scenario includes determining the denomination of U.S. currency in a transaction with no other observers present. Blind participants said they were most often concerned with scenarios involving taxis because they do not have a quick and easy way to confirm the value of the currency received in change. VI participants said the lighting in taxis is often not bright enough for them to be able to easily denominate currency. In these cash transactions, reliably knowing the denomination of the currency being given is as important as knowing the denomination of the currency being received.
- **Transactions while in a line, and receiving change.**
  Blind and VI participants described this scenario as one where they feel social pressure to complete the transaction quickly. Participants described this scenario as one where they would be more likely to put unknown notes in a separate pocket to sort later. However, participants noted that they feel there is greater chance of receiving incorrect change when no other people are present. Participants described instances where a bystander called attention to the fact that the participant was being given incorrect change.
- **Quick inventory of wallet or purse.**
  Blind and VI participants indicated that this activity was sometimes performed while in line and sometimes performed separately from a transaction.

Table 3-1. Focus Group Participants by Age

	5-17	18-64	65-79	80 and over	Totals
VI	2	33	15	7	57
Blind	3	43	7	3	56
Total	5	76	22	10	113

- **Sorting and organizing unknown notes – small quantities.**
  This scenario includes sorting and organizing unknown notes received as change in a transaction. Participants indicated that if they do not sort the notes immediately (e.g., because of time constraints or social pressure), they will typically get assistance from sighted acquaintances or use a reader device to sort the notes later.
- **Accepting cash for retail transactions.**
  This scenario involves blind and VI participants who work in retail or other cash-handling positions and deal with a large amount of cash each day (i.e., up to a thousand dollars). Half of all survey respondents (52% of the blind and 51% of the VI) work in such retail or other cash handling positions. Participants identified speed and accuracy as the key requirements for this scenario, with the focus on incoming cash (because outgoing cash is already sorted in the cash register).
- **Sorting and organizing unknown notes – large quantities.**
  Blind and VI participants who work with cash in retail or in the vending industry described this scenario as dealing with the cash after the store has closed for the day, or after removing cash from vending machines. In this scenario, the blind or VI person could be required to orient and sort large numbers of notes, so time and accuracy are both important.

Focus group participants identified three scenarios as the most important to them when handling currency—transactions with no other people in close proximity, transactions while in line (people waiting), and quick inventory of wallet or purse.

3.2.2. Existing Challenges

Focus group blind and VI participants discussed challenges in the denomination of U.S. currency. Participants reported using cash regularly (more than once a week). Focus group participants emphasized the importance of readily identifying currency denominations in every transaction. These findings were substantiated in the survey results (described in detail in Section 4), where participants reported using U.S. currency within an average of two days of taking the survey and over 90% of participants reported going out in public every day (see Section 4.2.2 for more survey information).

Blind and VI participants related instances where they were given incorrect change, usually not in their favor. Participants also described instances of having used the wrong denomination in a transaction. In many of the noted cases (both focus groups and surveys) the mistakes were unreported and discovered later, often at great inconvenience (e.g., not enough money for a future purchase). Participants at both the NFB and ACB focus groups reported being short- changed within days of the focus group discussion, with the most common scenario being in a taxi on the way to an airport or hotel. These findings were the same in the survey results (see Section 4), where 36% of the respondents reported that they had received incorrect change in the past year and 62% reported that they had given the wrong denominations in a transaction in the past year (see Section 4.2.2 for more survey information).

VI focus group participants said that the time required to correctly identify a currency denomination is very important to them. They reported that being able to denominate the note without having to hold the notes close to their eyes was also important, for ease of use, as well as to avoid social stigma.

VI focus group participants indicated that denominating most U.S. currency (i.e., $5, $10, $20, and $50 notes) does not require very much functional vision. They reported that recent changes, in particular large-print numerals (e.g., the larger purple numeral on the $5 note), have enabled faster and easier denomination. However, there are still some difficulties with the $50 and $20 notes, which can be confused because of the similar appearance of the numerals.

Focus group VI participants indicated that the $1 and $100 notes, which do not have the enlarged numeral, are considerably more difficult to denominate than the $5, $10, $20, and $50 notes. The participants said that they denominate these notes based on visual features other than the numerals. The most common features they use to denominate these notes are the light/dark pattern or silhouette, the portrait, or the word 'ONE' on the back of the $1 note. Difficulty denominating the $100 note was a common observation, though blind and VI participants both said that they do not often carry $100 notes.

The fear of being short-changed or of inadvertently giving someone the wrong note varied greatly among the focus group participants. Focus group participants who were concerned about the potential for being short-changed indicated that this concern is present for most transactions that involve strangers. The survey results (details in Section 4) echo these focus group comments: 72% of blind participants and 67% of VI participants said they felt vulnerable or disadvantaged using U.S. currency.

3.2.3. Common Adaptations

Focus group participants identified (1) sorting and folding beforehand, (2) using sighted assistance after the transaction, (3) using electronic note identifiers, and (4) choosing non-cash transactions as methods that they use to cope with difficulty denominating existing currency. Participants made it clear that, whichever method they used, security is their dominant concern.

Sorting Beforehand – Focus group participants stated that they sort and fold currency beforehand so that it can be extracted from a wallet or purse quickly. In some cases, participants said that they sort and fold their currency immediately upon receipt, with help either from the cashier or another sighted person. Other participants said they simply put unsorted notes aside to sort and fold later once they get home, either with assistance from a sighted person or a reader device.

Use of Technology – Focus group participants, particularly those who live alone, reported that electronic currency readers are useful for identifying currency when they return home. A few participants reported using flat-bed scanners, which are primarily designed for reading books and papers, to denominate unsorted currency. A few others reported using an Optacon (Optical Tactical Converter) to denominate currency. The Optacon is a discontinued optical scanning device that converts light and dark patterns into raised or lowered dots.

Alternate Methods of Payment – Blind and VI participants indicated that they use credit cards more frequently to avoid potential problems with cash transactions because this can give them confidence in the amount they are paying. However, the frequency of use of this strategy varied considerably among individuals and across different situations. Point-of-sale terminals are not considered accessible because they require sighted assistance. Most point-of-sale terminals have touch-screen interfaces and no audio capability, requiring blind and VI users to ask for assistance with entering a personal identification number (PIN), verifying the amount is correct, and with signature approval.

3.3. Conclusions – Needs and Challenges

More than one hundred blind and VI people participated in focus group sessions, including open forum discussions and small group sessions, to provide information about their experience with the use of U.S. currency. The following conclusions resulted from the focus group sessions:

- The three currency usage scenarios that are the most important to the participants are (1) transactions with no other people in close proximity, (2) transactions while in line (with people waiting), and (3) quick inventory of wallet or purse.
- Existing challenges for blind and VI people in the use of U.S. currency include (1) receiving the wrong denomination in change or providing the wrong denomination in a transaction, (2) social stigma caused by the time required for them to correctly identify a currency denomination, and (3) the potential for problems inherent in interactions with strangers.
- Adaptations to cope with existing currency for transactions include (1) sorting notes beforehand, (2) using sighted assistance after the transaction, (3) use of electronic note identifiers, and (4) choosing non-cash payment methods.

The information gathered in the focus group sessions was used to develop a survey to characterize vision-related difficulties with currency and to gain an understanding of how various currency accommodations might meet the needs of the blind and VI participants.

4. SURVEYS

4.1. Survey Objectives and Approach

The ARINC team compiled a survey of blind and VI people based on topics that arose in focus group sessions, ARINC team expertise, similar surveys conducted by the Bank of Canada, and advice from other sources such as the NCD. The objectives of the survey were to characterize vision-related difficulties with currency and to gain an understanding of how various currency accommodations might meet the needs of the blind and VI.

The ARINC team administered the survey as an email questionnaire (a few surveys were conducted via telephone interview upon participant request) and entered results into a database for analysis. Appendix C contains the survey questionnaire. To preserve participant anonymity, survey administrators did not retain the names of the individual respondents with the survey results.

The ARINC team analyzed results of the survey and categorized the results based on various segments of the blind and VI population. Section 4.2 includes highlights of the survey results and Appendix D includes the detailed survey results. The ARINC team calculated the survey margin of error for the survey blind population (sample size of 206) and the VI population (sample size of 196) as 0.0754 (+/- 7.5%) and 0.0886 (+/-8.9%), respectively. The margin of error is the maximum difference between the observed sample mean and the true value of the population mean. These calculations assume a standard normal distribution and a 95% degree of confidence. Wherever survey results are shown in this report, these margins of error apply.

4.2. Highlights of Survey Results

For the data shown in this section, the percentage values apply to all survey respondents except where noted in particular as blind or VI.

4.2.1. Participant Descriptions

The ARINC team solicited participation in the survey from individuals who visited the information table at the 2008 annual conventions of the ACB and the NFB. Volunteers provided contact information for administration of the survey, and an unknown number of these volunteers forwarded the survey to others in the blind and VI community, greatly expanding the geographic and demographic range of respondents beyond the attendees at the national conventions. Table 4-1 shows the number of survey participants by age group and whether they were blind or VI.

The survey results indicate that survey participants encompassed a wide demographic range; income levels ranged from less than $15,000 per year to more than $70,000 per year; living arrangements included living with a sighted person (47%), living alone (26%), and living with a blind person (22%). The remaining 5% included living with roommates or in a group facility, or no response. There were more females than males (57% females to 43% males), and participants from 49 states responded to the survey.

The ARINC team asked respondents to indicate the nature of their impairment to ascertain whether a particular set of responses might be linked with a common cause of vision impairment. Survey results indicate that the most common cause of vision impairment was retinopathy of prematurity (16%) followed by glaucoma (15%). Eleven percent of the respondents indicated "other," but listed a very wide range of diseases and conditions as the cause for their vision impairment. The majority of participants had one of 17 different causes for their vision impairment (see Appendix D, Survey Responses, for complete list); therefore, the ARINC team concluded that there was no single cause that could be linked with a particular set of responses.

Table 4-1. Survey Participants by Age

	5–17	18–64	65–79	80 and Over	None Given	Totals
VI	2	159	24	5	6	196
Blind	2	176	26	1	1	206
Total	4	335	50	6	7	402

4.2.2. Participant Reported Behavior

The survey results showed that the respondents are typically very active participants in the economy: 95% use a computer more than once a week; 90% go out in public more than once a week; 88% work; and 52% work with cash (retail, vending, etc.). On average, the respondents had used U.S. currency within two days of taking the survey.

The survey results show that respondents most frequently used the $1 denomination, followed by the $5, $20, and $10 denominations, respectively. The respondents used $2 denomination the least, followed by the $50 and $100 denominations, respectively.

Participants typically use a variety of technological devices: 89% use a cell phone (57% of all respondents have a phone with speech input or output features); 86% use a computer with a screen reader; 69% use a flatbed scanner; and 32% take a portable magnifier with them when they go out in public.

Most blind and VI survey participants indicated that they do not use a currency reader device, whether for work (76% said never), home (67% said never), or when they go out (83% said never). However, when asked if they would take a currency reader device with them if they had one, 36% responded that they would (27% said occasionally, 9% said frequently), while 41% said they would never take a device with them, and 23% said rarely.

4.2.3. Primary Participant Concerns

Confirming the concerns identified in the focus groups and open forums, 72% of the survey respondents indicated that they felt rushed during transactions, 72% said that they would feel less vulnerable if currency were easier for them to use, 70% felt vulnerable using cash, 62% gave someone incorrect denominations in a transaction in the past year, 60% indicated they would use currency more often if it was easier for them to use (in particular, avoiding the need for folding and sorting notes), 59% relied on someone at the point of sale to tell them what denominations they were receiving, and 36% of the participants believe they had received incorrect change in the past year.

4.2.4. Participant Attitudes toward Accommodations

Of the VI participants, 56% said that the large purple 5 on the new $5 note made it easier to identify the denomination (10% said it was more difficult). Sixteen percent of VI respondents said that the new background colors made it easier to identify the denomination, while seven percent said the background colors made it more difficult.

In response to a question on what accommodations they thought would be helpful, there were similar quantities of suggestions for a tactile accommodation (53% of all participants) as there were for note size differences (52% of all participants). Approximately 43% of the participants suggested more than one accommodation. A smaller percentage of participants suggested a larger high-contrast numeral (13%) or a tactile feature involving notched corners or perforations (10%). Finally, 4% of the survey respondents said that they did not want the BEP to make any changes to the current U.S. currency.

4.3. Conclusions – Survey of Vision Related Issues

The ARINC team conducted a survey to explore vision-related issues with U.S. currency. The survey was administered to 402 participants, 196 VI people and 206 blind people, with a broad geographic and demographic range. The survey yielded conclusions in the following areas:

Participant behavior:

- Survey respondents are active participants in the economy; they use computers regularly (95%), are active in their communities (90%), and work (88%).
- Respondents most frequently used the $1 currency denomination, followed by the $5, $20, and $10 denominations.
- Respondents typically use a wide variety of technological devices, including cell phones (89%), computer screen reader (86%), and flatbed scanners (69%).
- Respondents rarely use currency readers at work (76% never), home (67% never), or in public (83% never).
- When asked if they had a reader device, would they take it with them when they go out in public, 36% of respondents said that they would (27% occasionally, 9% frequently), 23% said rarely, and 41% said they would never take a device with them.

Primary concerns with currency use:

- Survey respondents feel rushed during transactions (72%).
- Respondents feel vulnerable using cash (70%).
- Respondents used incorrect denominations in a transaction within the past year (62%).
- Respondents rely on someone at the point of sale to tell them what denominations they were receiving (59%).

Accommodations:

- There was nearly the same percentage of participants who suggested a tactile accommodation (53%) as there was that suggested note size differences (52%).

5. TECHNICAL ANALYSIS OF ACCOMMODATIONS

An NRC study published in 1995[22] evaluated a number of different potential physical changes to U.S. currency, including note size changes, notched corners, holes, and tactile features to accommodate the needs of the blind. The NRC study also evaluated visual changes (including size of printed numerals), changes in predominant color, and changes in contrast of printed features to accommodate the needs of the VI. The NRC committee made the following recommendations, which are quoted directly from the report:

> "1) The committee recommends the use of size as a key to denomination, with or without the use of a size template.
>
> 2) The committee suggests evaluation of current approaches to size-denominated currency in other countries and determination of the magnitude of size differences that would make the six denominations sufficiently distinguishable.
>
> 3) The committee strongly recommends the use of large, high-contrast numerals on a uniform background.
>
> 4) The committee recommends the use of different predominant colors for the six denominations printed.
>
> 5) The committee considers coarse features to be secondary to the use of large, high-contrast numerals with a uniform background or color. These features would be useful if the portraits or other similar large, shaped patterns were distinctively located on the note."

Many factors impact the BEP's flexibility in modifying U.S. currency. A banknote's design will impact printing efficiency as well as the note's lifespan. Additionally, the note design must enhance the integrity of U.S. currency through a variety of counterfeit deterrent features. The BEP cannot compromise these features when considering a currency redesign. Moreover, the BEP must comply with several statutory requirements: 12 U.S.C. § 413 requires that banknotes bear serial numbers assigned by the Federal Reserve Board of Governors; 12 U.S.C. § 418 requires that the numbers of the issuing Federal Reserve Banks be printed on the notes; and 31 U.S.C. § 5114(b) requires that *In God We Trust* be printed on all U.S. banknotes. Finally, while not a statutory requirement, the signatures of the Secretary of the Treasury and the Treasurer of the United States have been included on all U.S. currency for many years.

In this section, the ARINC team has augmented the previous technical analysis to provide the information needed to evaluate implementation of currency features and accommodations for blind and VI people. The objective of the technical analysis was to understand the challenges associated with each potential feature, not to make recommendations. This technical analysis was focused on understanding the practical implementation of the various features. The ARINC team gathered information using the following sources:

- **Countries that have implemented features**. The team contacted individuals who could provide an understanding of the rationale for incorporating certain features and identify problems encountered during the implementation period.
- **Subject Matter Experts**. The team contacted subject matter experts and scientists with expertise related to the various technical features or researchers who regularly work with blind and VI people.
- **Industry Stakeholders.** The team contacted individuals in the business community who would be working with new features in daily cash transactions.
- **Equipment Manufacturers.** The team contacted companies that presently produce cash handling and processing equipment to understand equipment parameters and limitations. The questions used to initiate discussions are included in Appendix E.

- **Government Organizations.** The team contacted the Currency Technology Office (CTO), the technical arm of the Federal Reserve System's Cash Product Office (CPO). The CTO supports the Federal Reserve Board (FRB) high speed currency processing function. The team also met with the U.S. Secret Service for information on how different accommodations would affect their processes.

The potential impact of implementation of currency features on the FRB operations is a key consideration. As the central bank of the U.S., the FRB serves as the bankers' bank, helping to assure the safety and efficiency of the payments system, and as the Government's bank, processing a variety of transactions involving trillions of dollars. As the FRB receives cash deposits from commercial banks, it counts and authenticates the currency and removes worn or damaged notes from circulation. The U.S. Treasury uses the FRB to handle incoming federal tax deposits and outgoing Government payments and to sell and redeem U.S. Government securities such as savings bonds and Treasury bills, notes, and bonds. The FRB controls the nation's cash supply by distributing coin and currency produced by the BEP and the U.S. Mint to financial institutions.

The findings of the technical analysis of currency features were grouped into five general categories—numeral size changes, color changes, machine-readable features, tactile features, and note size changes.

5.1. Numeral Size Changes

Numeral size changes have been implemented to address the key scenarios for VI people for denominating currency (i.e., quick inventory and public transactions). Accessibility of larger numerals for VI people is supported by clinical studies, research into visual perception science, prior NRC studies, and experience, both in the U.S. and internationally.[23][24][25] The 1995 NRC Report contains a detailed discussion of the numeral sizes, *viz.*

> "The use of large, high-contrast numerals on a simple, uniform background can provide an effective means to enable visually disabled people to more easily denominate notes. "Large" here refers to numerals greater than 40 percent of the full height of the current banknote...
>
> ...This size would be well within the limit of people with acuity of 20/160 or better for viewing bills at a distance of one meter, which is roughly the distance from the eye to the checkout counter of a grocery store, enabling easy and rapid identification...
>
> ...If the numeral were 60 percent of the current banknote height, it would serve people with acuity as low as 20/240 in the same situation. Moreover, the large, easy-to-read numerals would be recognizable by people with extremely low acuities (less than 20/1000) if bills were held at a normal reading distance of 40 cm (16 inches). Numerals of this size would be substantially larger than those on current U.S. banknotes. Large numerals are not needed on all four corners, but it would be preferable that one large numeral be included on each side of the banknote."

A subject matter expert in optometry[26] contacted by the ARINC team supported the NRC analysis. However, the subject matter expert cautioned that there is a wide variety of visual impairments and that numeral size changes would not be an ideal solution for all groups (e.g.,

VI people with age-related macular degeneration). As noted in Section 3.2.2, VI focus group participants said the large purple 5 on the back of the new U.S. $5 note enabled faster and easier denomination. However, when VI survey participants were asked if the new $5 note design affected their ability to identify the denomination, 56% said it was easier, but 10% said it was more difficult.

Three of the major cash-handling machine manufacturers (in terms of market share) surveyed for this study said that replacement or adjustment of existing sensors and software programming would be required to implement different sized numerals to meet end user needs. The manufacturers suggested that these changes could be accomplished in less than one year. However, all three voiced concern about the change-over process and the need to accommodate both old and new notes of several different denominations. The FRB CTO[27] noted that the change-over process is critical to the complexity of accommodating a new design. The CTO also indicated that inspection of new printed features may require development of new sensors, with an approximate 3-year time frame to implement.

5.2. Color Changes

Using different primary colors for different denominations addresses the key usage scenarios for denominating currency for VI people (i.e., quick inventory and public transactions). This accommodation allows denomination without the individual having to fully remove the notes from a wallet. This feature would benefit most VI groups, with the possible exception of those with color vision impairment, depending on the colors chosen.

Clinicians at the New England College of Optometry[28] and at the University of California at Berkeley[29] with recognized experience in color perception and color vision impairment, respectively, indicated that color plays a secondary role compared to contrast. They suggested that additional color features are less likely to benefit VI people than features with high luminance or high contrast. Thus, while predominant color changes may be of primary value for a subset of the VI population, contrast of features such as numerals appears to have a much greater impact, especially for those who have color perception impairment. VI participants in the survey reported a wide variety of color pairs that were difficult to tell apart, with 44% of all VI participants reporting that they have color vision problems.

The FRB CTO indicated that significant changes in color, either the primary color of the note or introduction of a colored feature, could require either new sensors or reprogramming of authentication machines. They estimated it could take as long as three years for these types of changes and that this could require significant capital investment.

Three of the largest cash-handling machine manufacturers (in terms of market share) surveyed for this study, along with personnel from the corporate offices of a large commercial bank (top five in terms of assets), indicated that printed features such as higher contrast colors would primarily require sensor changes and software programming to support implementation. As with the similar changes for numeral size, the manufacturers said that these changes could be accomplished throughout the industry in less than one year but that the need to support old and new notes of several different denominations simultaneously could be a challenge.

5.3. Machine-Readable Features

Machine-readable features have been investigated for both blind and VI people to address the key usage scenarios (i.e., quick inventory and public transactions). The effect of paper manufacturing processes on the detection accuracy of a machine-readable feature is an implementation risk for a device that depends on light transmission. However, new machine-readable features could enable manufacturers to develop new currency reader device technologies that blind and VI people might be more inclined to use (see Section 4.2.2 for survey participant perceptions of devices).

Large banknote counting machines, such as those used at the FRB and in banking operations, employ machine-readable features as part of their high speed authentication or counting process. One machine-readable feature is magnetic ink, where each denomination generates a distinctive magnetic field. Another such feature, with fluorescent properties, can be detected by ultraviolet scanning technology. Sensitive digital cameras, such as those employed on cell phone currency readers, can reference the optical patterns in notes against a database of authentic patterns. The ARINC team did not identify any handheld devices employing machine-readable features that have been developed on a commercial scale. Although there is a Canadian currency reader device provided by the Canadian government, it was not developed on a commercial scale and is not available to the general public. Potential manufacturers indicated that the unknown size of a commercial market is a limiting factor in development of such a device.

5.4. Raised Profile Features

Raised-profile tactile features would address the key usage scenarios (i.e., quick inventory and public transaction) for both blind and VI people.

In order to benchmark the international experience with raised-profile tactile features, the ARINC team interviewed the ECB Director of Banknotes and an analyst with the Bank of Canada. The Bank of Canada and the ECB use similar embossing methods to create tactile features. The Canadian process includes filling in the indentations on the opposite side of the feature with a durable resin. The height of the feature is limited by the bursting strength of the paper. The limits on the height of an embossed feature and variability in height due to normal variations in paper formation have not been established.

The Canadian design uses a pattern of circular bumps, which grew out of early efforts to use Braille as a tactile feature. The Bank of Canada consulted with a respected Queens University tactile expert in the currency design process. The tactile expert suggested that material tactile features (e.g., texture) are preferable to geometric features (e.g., size or shape) because the sense of touch can detect and analyze material features more accurately and faster than geometric features. Other currencies, such as the euro, have raised bars for a tactile feature. However these tactile features lose their effectiveness once they have been widely circulated and the features become less prominent.

Manufacturers of cash-handling machines surveyed for this study said that, based on their experience with the tactile features on new Canadian notes (140 microns), they could accommodate features of that height. Features higher than the Canadian note feature would require more research to determine feasibility. One of the three largest manufacturers (in terms of market share), along with personnel from the corporate offices of a large commercial bank (top five in terms of assets), voiced concern that raised features would adversely affect stacking, mechanical counting, examination, and finishing processes.

The FRB CTO indicated that a tactile feature 160 microns or less in height was considered easily accommodated, since the total height change in a bundle would be similar to that accommodated with the insertion of security threads into U.S. currency.

5.5. Notched Corners and Perforations/Holes

Notched corners and perforations would address the key usage scenarios (i.e., quick inventory and public transactions) for both blind and VI people. Under most scenarios, the user would still have to remove the notes from the wallet or billfold to denominate using these tactile features (e.g., checking all four corners).

The process of creating notched or perforated tactile features creates waste because material is removed, regardless of when the process is performed. If the feature is created prior to the printing operation, there is potential for surface contamination and resultant print and image defects. The risk of printing process contamination would be mitigated if the feature is created after the notes are printed. However, the potential effects of contamination on downstream converting and mechanical operations, and the effect of holes on note lifetime will need to be determined. The Vice President and General Manager of Crane & Co., Inc., the manufacturer of U.S. currency paper, said that introducing holes, perforations, or notched corners in their manufacturing process would be a potential source of surface contamination of the sheeted product that is shipped to BEP. Manufacturing personnel at BEP have similar quality control concerns if the feature is added during the printing operation.

Manufacturers of cash-handling machines for commercial use said that these tactile features would require programming changes to account for the light transmitted through various portions of the notes. They estimated that changes could be made in less than one year, assuming that the rest of the current design is unchanged. This estimate for changes in sensors and sensor design is significantly shorter than what would appear to be comparable sensor changes that would be required by the CTO (approximately three to seven years, depending on the nature of the feature). The difference between the two timeframes can be traced to the level of sophistication of the two types of machines. The CTO counting and authentication equipment runs at higher processing speeds, and are held to a much higher level of accuracy than typical commercial cash handling machines.

Both domestic and international banking representatives predict significant negative effects on both manual and mechanical processing of notes with notches or perforations. Commercial banking representatives predicted significant jams of mechanical equipment requiring additional units to be purchased to offset productivity losses and substantially increased maintenance requirements. Manual processing was also expected to see a productivity drop as worn or mutilated notes could become entangled. Finally a concern was expressed that notches or holes would propagate tears with the ultimate result of decreased note lifetime.

5.6. Note Size Changes

Varying note size by denomination would address the key usage scenarios (i.e., quick inventory and public transactions) for blind and VI people. Half of the survey participants said that they thought notes of different sizes would make the currency easier to denominate. Depending on the size variation format used, blind people may still need to remove a note from their wallet to accurately identify the denomination. The longer this determination takes the less desirable this option would be in a public transaction setting.

Size changes can be implemented along one or two dimensions of the note. The 1995 NRC report discusses the denomination accuracy rates of both options for blind users. According to that report, a 12 mm change in one dimension for each denomination results in a significantly lower accuracy rate of only 75% compared to a 90% accuracy rate[30] when note sizes were changed in both dimensions; length by 7 mm and height by 5 mm for each denomination.

Many countries vary note size by denomination,[31] as does the European Union (EU). Both length and width of the euro vary proportionally by denomination, while other currencies, such as the Australian dollar, only vary in one dimension.

The ARINC team investigated the impact size changes (i.e., variation of either one or two size dimensions) would have on cash-handling processes across U.S. Government and commercial organizations. As indicated in the following responses, modified or replacement hardware for counting and authentication may be required at every step where these devices are employed in both Government and commercial processes.

- Crane & Co., Inc. indicated that a change in sizes of the notes would not likely have significant impact on their operations, either on the paper machines or the sheeting operation.
- The BEP indicated that new printing and processing equipment planned for installation could handle different sizes of notes as long as the size differences did not exceed the maximum size (181 mm by 74 mm) of the largest Swiss notes (1000 Swiss francs).
- The FRB CTO indicated that size changes would significantly affect all of their machines, vault space, and working areas and at least temporarily increase manpower while staff became accustomed to working with the new sizes. The FRB CTO estimated that it could take as long as seven years to make these changes. The most sophisticated counting and authentication equipment, held to the highest accuracy standard, is located in Federal Reserve Banks and branches throughout the country. While small in total quantity, the design lead time and capital costs for this equipment could be substantial.
- Personnel from the corporate offices of a large commercial bank (top five in terms of assets) predicted that a three- to five-year transition with major capital investment in high-speed cash processing equipment would be required for note size changes. Commercial banks typically have one or more centralized high-speed operations within each metropolitan area that they serve. These centers are used for counting and authentication operations for all of the branches in the region in preparation for exchanges with the CTO. This instrumentation is held to a much higher standard of accuracy with commensurate increases in design lead time and manufacturing costs.

While not as numerous as the number of bank branches, the number of commercial banking high-speed operations is in the hundreds.

- Three of the largest cash-handling machine manufacturers (in terms of market share) surveyed for this study indicated that they have developed the required technology and experience to accommodate note size variation by producing machinery for the European market. The cash machine manufacturers estimated that 12–24 months would be required to change cash-handling hardware in their end-user customer locations.

- From an implementation perspective, dimension changes in commercial cash handling will affect the greatest number of people and businesses since cash drawers in hundreds of thousands of retail locations might have to be modified or replaced to accommodate new note sizes. Also, vending applications that accept a range of denominations in a variety of commercial sectors such as gambling, transportation, and transit, would require modification to accept different note sizes or to limit the number of denominations they accept. Generally, these vending machine applications are held to the lowest standard of authentication accuracy; design and manufacture do not represent significant equipment development challenges; however the equipment quantity nationwide is in the millions. Costs to upgrade the equipment on an absolute basis are not high, but would eventually have to be incurred by someone, and the impact could still be significant on a relative basis depending upon the size of the business required to bear the costs.

European organizations have indicated that the magnitude of capital investment and lead time were not as significant for them to accommodate note size variance in the euro because the infrastructure to accommodate different sizes already existed in Europe.

5.7. Conclusions – Technical Analysis of Accommodations

The ARINC team performed a technical analysis focused on the practical implementation of currency features for blind and VI people. Five major features were analyzed:

- Numeral size changes are a proven means to address quick inventory and public transaction scenarios for VI people. Fifty-six percent of VI survey respondents said the new large purple 5 on the back of the new U.S. $5 note enabled faster and easier denomination.

- Primary color changes for different denominations are options to address quick inventory and public transaction scenarios for VI people. While predominant color changes may be of value for a subset of the VI population, increasing the contrast of features, such as numerals, would provide greater benefit.

- Machine-readable features have promise for development of new devices for both blind and VI people for quick inventory and public transactions.

- Raised-profile tactile features including raised dots have been introduced in Canada and are effective, especially for blind people. However these tactile features lose their effectiveness once they have been widely circulated and the features become less prominent. Industrial users and manufacturers are concerned with the effect of raised features on stacking, mechanical counting, and authentication processes.

- The introduction of tactile features such as holes, perforations, or notched corners in the manufacturing process could cause surface contamination that could adversely affect downstream processing.
- A number of countries (e.g., including the United Kingdom (UK), Sweden, Switzerland, and Australia), and the EU vary note size by denomination. Introduction of size changes without an existing infrastructure would require significantly modified hardware for counting and authentication at every step where these devices are employed in both Government and commercial processes.

6. USABILITY TESTING

The objective of the usability testing described in this section was to measure how well the available accessibility accommodations (both currency features and currency reader devices) accomplish their intended purpose. The usability tests focused on the following questions:

- Does the accommodation allow blind or VI people to accurately denominate currency?
- How quickly can blind or VI people denominate currency using the accommodation?
- What is the error rate (denomination incorrectly identified by participant)?
- What are the differences between the blind and VI groups?

The ARINC team administered usability testing with volunteer participants attending the annual conferences of the ACB and NFB, volunteer adult participants at the Blind Industries and Services of Maryland, volunteer student participants at the Perkins School for the Blind, as well as others at the following locations:

- Richmond, Virginia (retirement center and participants' homes)
- Boston, Massachusetts (participants' homes)
- Baltimore, Maryland (city-run drop-in senior center, and participants' homes)
- Hartford, Connecticut (retirement center and participants' homes)
- Washington, DC greater metropolitan area (service organizations and participants' homes)

Test administrators used a common test method as shown in the box below. The usability testing focused on task-based performance in denominating notes from a set of known choices. The ARINC team emphasized measuring and comparing the relative performance of existing notes that incorporate accommodations for the blind and VI. However, the usability of different features is subjective (i.e., a matter of personal preference).

USABILITY TEST METHOD

- Explain the goals of the study to the participant emphasizing that this is a test of the materials (including the currency), and not a test of their skills or competence.
- Demonstrate how to use each feature or device, and then let the participants conduct training/familiarization trials.
- Provide the participants with samples of currency features or one of the devices, and then ask the participant to use the feature or device and report the denomination of each note. (For this task the objective was to gather accuracy and speed data, as well as subjective impressions and willingness to use the feature or device.)
- Ask the participant to determine if the tested accommodation is useful in the key scenarios.
- Repeat tests for each of the accommodations.

6.1. Participants

Table 6-1 provides the range of ages and vision impairment for the usability test participants. Appendix F contains the list of participant profiles. Appendix G provides the usability test procedures and script. Appendix H provides comments from the U.S. and international currency usability testing and Appendix I provides comments from the reader devices and prototype currency features usability testing.

6.2. Usability Testing Results for Devices

The ARINC team evaluated three commercially available currency reader devices in usability tests with blind participants—two devices that require the user to slide the note into the device and a cell phone camera. In addition, the team evaluated three developmental prototypes—two devices that require the user to slide the note into the device and a cell phone camera. The results of usability testing for prototype devices were included in this study, even though the manufacturers may make changes to the devices that would change the test outcomes before the production devices are offered to the public. Pricing information is included in Section 8.7.1. For the prototypes, the manufacturers provided an estimated cost, but emphasized that the final price would change based on design changes or estimated market size.

The ARINC team conducted usability testing on currency reader devices that were operational during the time period between June 2008 and April 2009. The reader device industry continues to introduce new devices as technological breakthroughs are realized. For example, several participants indicated that having the option of an earphone or wireless notification option would be a potential benefit in that people around them would not hear a verbal notification of the value of the currency; this type of technology may be incorporated new devices.

Consumer electronics advance through their product lifecycles (from introduction through maturity to obsolescence) at a rapid rate. When new technology is introduced in commercial products, procurement or acquisition costs can be initially high and then decrease as the product matures in the market. Classic examples are advances in cell phones, personal digital assistants, and Global Positioning System (GPS) equipment.

Sections 6.2.1 through 6.2.6 include descriptions of the individual devices and results from the usability testing. Section 6.2.7 contains a summary of the conclusions of the device usability testing. The averages of accuracy and speed discussed in the narratives of Sections 6.2.1 through 6.2.6 represent the summary results from the total participants for all trials of each device. Because the figures in Section 6.2.1 through 6.2.6 (Figures 6-1 through 6-12) represent the average results for each trial individually, a calculation to average these average data points will not yield the exact same results as the narratives.

6.2.1. Commercial Device #1, Slide-in Reader #1

The first device was a slide-in note reader, designated as Slide-in #1. This device has a rectangular shape with approximate dimensions of 3 in. x 6 in. x 1 in. To use the device, the user simply slides the note into a slot in the top surface. The device activates automatically when the note is inserted and identifies the note with voice annunciation.

The test administrators observed that this device was very easy to use for almost all of the test participants, and required very little training (average of 183 seconds). The results of the usability tests, shown in Figures 6-1 and 6-2, show an average accuracy of 98% for blind participants. However, the device took an average of 21.7 seconds to correctly denominate each note. In general, the device error rate increased as battery power decreased, but infrequent errors still occurred even with fresh batteries.

The test administrators noted the following subjective comments and observations from the participants with respect to Slide-in #1:

- Most participants said that the device was too large to carry with them when shopping.
- A few participants said that they already owned this device, or one like it.
- Participants who said they might be potential users noted the price of a device could be a limiting factor.

Table 6-1. Usability Testing Participants by Age

	5–17	18–64	65–79	80 and Over	Totals
VI	5	23	4	10	42
Blind	17	47	19	11	94
Total	22	70	23	21	136

- Participants who owned the device complained about the device denomination accuracy. They reported that the device had a significant number of "cannot read" responses and occasional false-positives for other denominations.

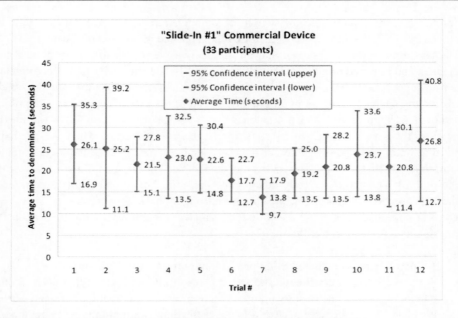

Figure 6-1. Commercial Device #1 - Blind Participant Average Times (seconds).

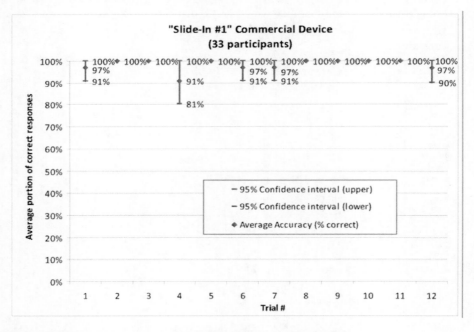

Figure 6-2. Commercial Device #1 - Blind Participant Average Accuracy.

6.2.2. Commercial Device #2, Slide-in Reader #2

The second device was a slide-in note reader, functionally very similar to Slide-in #1 and designated as Slide-in #2. This device has a rectangular shape with approximate dimensions of 3 in. x 3 in. x 1 in. and a selector switch for annunciation type (voice, tone, or vibration). The device detects a machine-readable feature that is present at one end of the note.

The test administrators observed that this device was very easy to use for almost all test participants, and required minimal training (average of 140 seconds). Participants often had to attempt different note orientations to identify the denomination because the machine-readable feature that the device reads is only present at one end of the note. The results of the usability tests, shown in Figures 6-3 and 6-4, indicate an average accuracy of 98% for the blind participants, the same as Slide-in #1. All observed errors occurred when the participants inserted the notes slightly off-center; it appeared that the machine-readable code could be misinterpreted in these cases. However, the device was faster than Slide-in #1, with an average of 17.3 seconds to correctly denominate the note. This included the time needed to turn the note around and make a second attempt in roughly half of the trials.

The test administrators noted the following subjective comments and observations from the participants with respect to Slide-in #2:

- All participants considered Slide-in #2 more portable than Slide-in #1.
- Some participants considered the speed of use to be an issue, although it is unclear whether this was due to slow optimal reaction time or the fact that in many cases the user had to turn the note over or rotate it (sometimes multiple times) to get a positive reading.
- Some participants said that they would prefer that slide-in devices read notes inserted with any orientation because turning notes around was very tedious and time-consuming.

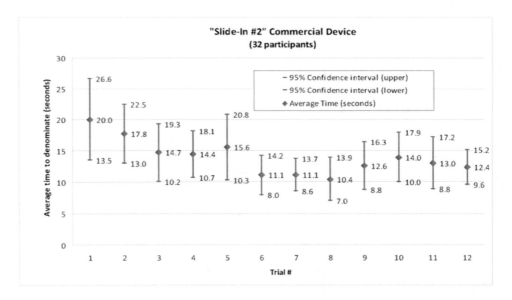

Figure 6-3. Commercial Device #2 - Blind Participant Average Times (seconds).

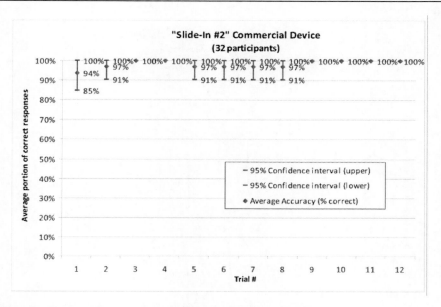

Figure 6-4. Commercial Device #2 - Blind Participant Average Accuracy.

- Some participants had a positive response to the switchable readout, including voice output (preferred at home) and tones or vibrations (preferred in public).
- Participants had difficulty inserting the most widely circulated notes into the device. The insertion force required to press the note into the slot occasionally caused the notes to fold over and thus not properly activate the switch.

6.2.3. Commercial Device #3, Cell Phone Reader #1

The third device tested was a cell phone (containing a camera) with a currency-reading software application. This device has a rectangular shape with approximate dimensions of 2 in. x 4.4 in. x 0.7 in. This application is initiated with the press of one button. To read a note, the user holds the cell phone camera at a specific height over the note, presses a single button on the cell phone, waits for a click sound (simulated camera shutter), then waits for a verbal annunciation (e.g., either the denomination or an error message). If there was an error message it was retested adding to the overall test time. A few participants already owned this device and noted that they were likely to be carrying it for reasons other than for currency denomination, in most cases to read text on documents or items, or as an accessible cell phone for making or receiving calls.

The test administrators observed that this device was moderately easy to use for most participants and took slightly more training time than the slide-in devices (average of 251 seconds). The participants generally required a few attempts to get used to the device's ergonomic requirements. The results of the usability tests, shown in Figures 6-5 and 6-6, indicate that the average accuracy of 100% for blind participants was the best of all the devices. However, the device was slower than the slide-in models, with an average speed of 34.2 seconds to correctly denominate the note (almost twice the average time measured for Slide-in #2).

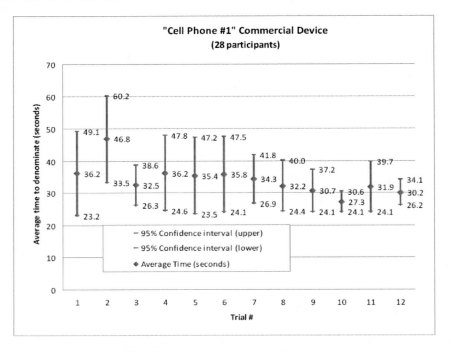

Figure 6-5. Commercial Device #3 - Blind Participant Average Times (seconds).

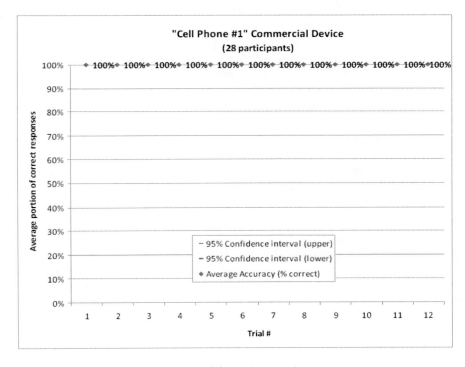

Figure 6-6. Commercial Device #3 - Blind Participant Average Accuracy.

Some participants needed more practice attempts than others before successfully completing on their own. In particular, all participants needed a period to practice (1) aiming the cell phone properly (with sufficient distance, and parallel to the note), (2) pressing a tiny trigger button on the keypad (many inadvertently pressed an adjacent button) to snap a shot, and (3) keeping fingers out of the way of the lens. Most participants found the device easy to use once they learned these nuances.

The test administrators noted the following subjective comments and observations from the participants with respect to the cell phone reader:

- Most participants believed that the system would be too slow for use in public, but might be useful at home.
- Most participants said that the need to use a flat surface, and to have both hands free, would make the device difficult to use while in line.

6.2.4. Prototype Device #1, Slide-in Reader #3

The first prototype device tested was a slide-in note reader, designated as 'Slide-in #3.' This device has a rectangular shape with approximate dimensions of 2.8 in x 1.6 in x 0.75 in. and a selector switch for annunciation type (voice, tone, or vibration). To use the device, the user was required to slide the note into a slot in the top (largest) surface and press one of the buttons on the end (smallest surface). The device identified the note a few seconds after insertion. All testing was conducted using the voice annunciation from the available output modes.

The test administrators observed that this device was easy to use for most test participants with good dexterity, and required little training (average of 177 seconds). Some older participants had difficulty with note insertion and with finding the button on the side of the device. The results of the usability tests, shown in Figures 6-7 and 6-8, indicate that this device had the second-highest accuracy of all the devices tested, at 99%, and was nearly as fast as Slide-in #2. The only false- positive (misread value) errors observed occurred when the note was inserted with a corner folded over. The device performed quickly, with an average of 17.6 seconds to correctly denominate each note.

The test administrators noted the following subjective comments and observations from the participants with respect to Slide-in #3:

- Most participants believed that the system would be small enough to carry with them when they go shopping or out to a restaurant, and might be useful in some cases (for example, verifying notes left as a restaurant tip).
- Only a few participants said they thought the device would be fast enough for verifying change while standing in line, but others suggested that they would step aside and use the device while remaining within the general area of the cashier in case there was a discrepancy.

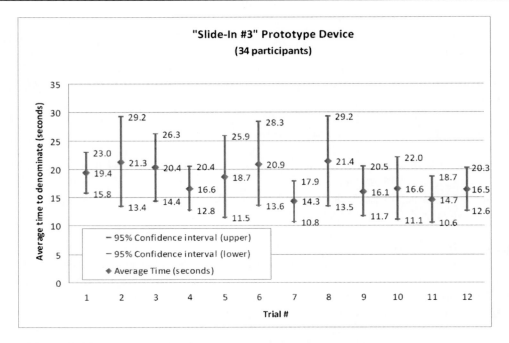

Figure 6-7. Prototype Device #1 - Blind Participant Average Times (seconds).

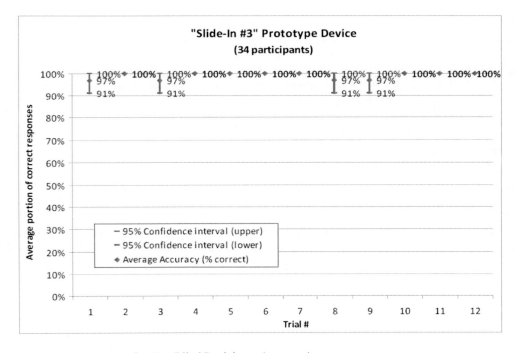

Figure 6-8. Prototype Device #1 - Blind Participant Average Accuracy.

6.2.5. Prototype Device #2, Cell Phone Reader #2

The second prototype device tested was a cell phone (containing a camera) with a currency- reader software application. This software application is intended to operate on any typical cell- phone, therefore, specific dimensions were not provided. The user initiates the reader application with three taps on the screen, which is a temporary method for the prototype only. To identify currency, the user held the camera cell phone over the note at a specific distance and orientation, and awaited the voice annunciation of the denomination. Once the software had been activated, the user did not need to press any buttons to initiate the device.

The test administrators observed that the requirement to determine the correct distance and orientation between the device and the note made this device difficult to use for most participants and impossible for some. Specifically, the test administrators observed that it was difficult for some participants to hold one object (the note) in one hand in an exact position relative to another object (the phone) in the other hand, as recommended by the device developer. The device took significantly longer for training than any of the other devices (average of 319 seconds). Performance in this task varied greatly among blind participants, with no apparent correlation with age or how long the participant had been blind. Even participants who reported having very good spatial awareness had difficulty using this device.

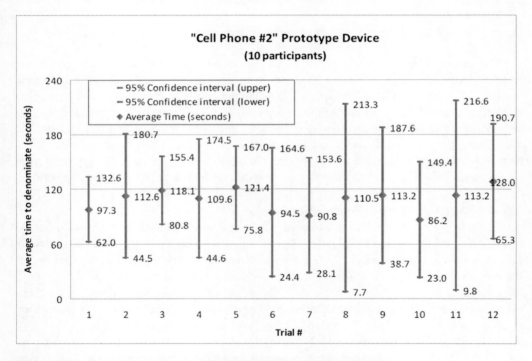

Figure 6-9. Prototype Device #2 - Blind Participant Average Times (seconds).

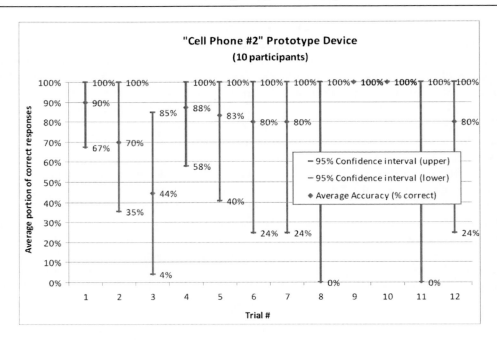

Figure 6-10. Prototype Device #2 - Blind Participant Average Accuracy.

The results of the usability tests, shown in Figures 6-9 and 6-10, indicate that this device had the lowest accuracy (average of 76%) of all the devices tested and took the longest time (average of 102.5 seconds) to correctly denominate the note. The device also had the highest number of misread values of any of the devices tested. Many trials were terminated because the participant grew frustrated after two or three minutes without successful identification. In these cases, the trial was discontinued and recorded as an error. The quantity of participants that were able to test this device is lower than the others because of these discontinued trials (some participants did not want to begin testing once they had completed the training period).

6.2.6. Prototype Device #3, Note Corner Reader

The third prototype device tested was an imaging device that uses the corner of a note to identify the denomination. The device shape is longer and narrower than the commercially available devices, approximately 2 in. x 4 in. x 1.5 in. To operate the device, the user inserts the corner of the note into a slot at one end and presses a button in the middle of the device to trigger recognition. The device announces the value of the note with a pattern of beeps between one and three seconds after insertion. The device was designed to allow recognition from any note corner for all U.S. currency denominations currently in circulation.

The test administrators observed that many blind participants had difficulty inserting the notes with the required precision because a groove near the actual insertion slot felt like the insertion slot. The senior and elderly participants had more difficulty holding the note square in the slot and operating the trigger button, which did not provide sufficient feedback to the user when pressed. Several participants noted that the device required two hands for use.

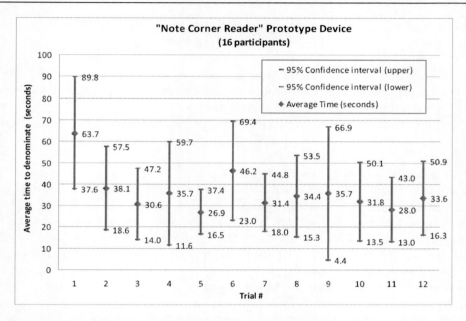

Figure 6-11. Prototype Device #3 - Blind Participant Average Times (seconds).

The note corner reader had an average training time of 201 seconds. The results of the usability tests, shown in Figures 6-11 and 6-12, indicate that this device had the second-lowest accuracy (average of 81%) of all the devices tested. The device was also one of the slower devices, taking an average of 36.5 seconds to correctly identify the denomination.

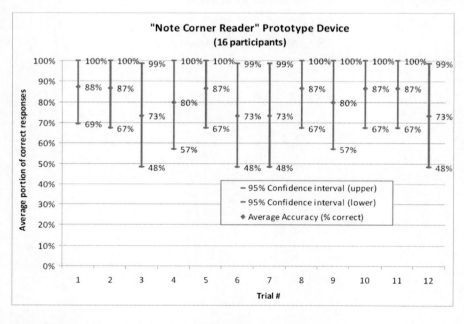

Figure 6-12. Prototype Device #3 - Blind Participant Average Accuracy.

The test administrators noted the following subjective comments and observations from the participants with respect to the prototype imaging device:

- Some participants said that the beeps indicating denomination were too fast.
- Most participants indicated that a voice output mode would be preferred (this feature is planned but was not available at the time of this test).
- A few participants preferred the portability of the note corner reader device relative to Slide-in #1, but not relative to the smaller Slide-in devices #2 and #3.

6.2.7. Conclusions – Device Usability Testing

The ARINC team performed usability testing on six currency reader devices that were operational at the time of the usability testing, between June 2008 and April 2009. Three of the devices were commercial products and three were developmental prototypes that the manufacturers made available for this study. The number of participants is lower for some devices because the participants chose not to continue with that device after receiving the training, or after an initial set of trials.

Figures 6-13 and 6-14 show the summary results across all six devices. Figure 6-13 shows the average time (at the 95% confidence interval) for a participant to correctly identify the currency denomination using each device. Average recognition speed was the measure of time beginning when the participant took the reader in hand and ending when the participant declared the denomination. Figure 6-14 shows the average accuracy of the devices. Each test participant was presented with each denomination multiple times within each test. Participants scored one for correct identification and zero for incorrect identification for each denomination. In general, the tests show that the devices are highly accurate, but infrequently the devices would identify the denomination incorrectly.

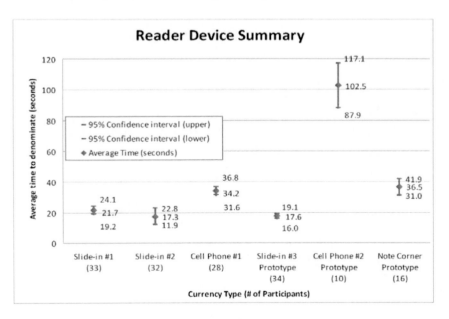

Figure 6-13. All Devices - Blind Participant Average Times (seconds).

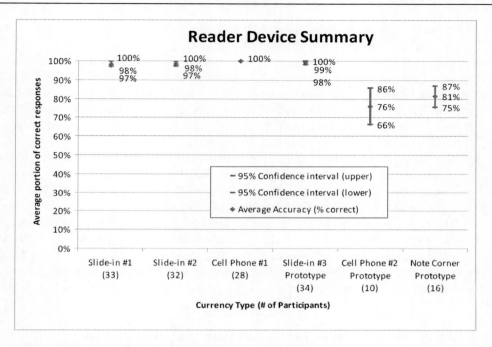

Figure 6-14. All Devices - Blind Participant Average Accuracy.

Figures 6-13 and 6-14 present results summarized for each device in the usability testing. Because the average accuracy and speed results in Figures 6-13 and 6-14 are the averages of the total participant results for all trials of each device, a calculation to average the average data points presented in Figures 6-1 through 6-12 will not yield the exact same results as Figures 6-13 and 6-14.

The usability tests of reader devices by blind participants yielded the following conclusions:

- Test participants cited accuracy, portability, and speed of use as the most important factors in their willingness to use a reader device.
- Slide-in #1 was easy for the test participants to learn and use. This device had an average speed to accurately denominate notes of 21.7 seconds (slower than Slide-in #2 and #3). The device error rate increased as battery power decreased, but infrequent errors still occurred even with fresh batteries. Overall accuracy was 98%. Participants said that the device was too large to carry with them for public transactions.
- Slide-in #2 was easy for the test participants to learn and use. The device correctly denominated the note in an average time of 17.3 seconds. Test participants said that the portability and switchable output modes were preferred over Slide-in #1.
- Slide-in #3 was easy for most test participants to learn and use, but some participants who had dexterity impairments had more difficulty. The device correctly denominated the note in an average time of 17.6 seconds, very close to the time for Slide-in #2. Test participants liked the device's portability, accuracy, and speed

(roughly a third of the participants said they might be willing to use it for transactions while in line).

- The commercial cell phone reader #1 was moderately easy to use for most participants, highly accurate (average 100%) but provided slow results. The device had an average first-use training time of 251 seconds and correctly denominated the note in an average of 34.2 seconds. Test participants said that this device was not fast enough for use in public, but might be useful for home use (where speed is not as much of an issue) because of its high accuracy rate.
- The prototype note corner reader was a bit slower than the commercial cell-phone reader, with an average time to correctly identify the denomination of 36.5 seconds. The accuracy was not as good as the other devices, with an average of 81%. Most participants said they would not use this device, even at home.
- The prototype cell-phone reader was difficult to use, in some cases taking several minutes to correctly identify a denomination, with an average time to identify of 102.5 seconds. Several participants declined to test this device after the training period. The low accuracy rate of 76% is primarily a result of participants giving up after several minutes of not being able to get the device to identify a note.

6.3. Usability Testing Results for U.S. and International Currency

The ARINC team conducted usability testing for U.S. currency, six foreign currencies, and test notes featuring prototype accommodations. The purpose of these tests was to establish the effectiveness of different features in the various currency designs. A detailed description of the U.S. and foreign currency features is included in Appendix J.

Test results are reported separately for blind and VI users in terms of recognition speed and recognition accuracy with 95% confidence intervals for each set of measurements. The ARINC team measured average recognition speed beginning when the participant took the note in hand and ending when the participant declared the denomination.

The ARINC team computed the average recognition accuracy. Each test participant was presented with each denomination multiple times within each test. Participants scored one for correct identification and zero for incorrect identification for each denomination. For example, if a participant examined a note three times and identified it correctly twice, the score would be 67% (2/3) accuracy.

The ARINC team averaged accuracy and speed results across all participants to ensure that the variable number of exposures, individual participant variation in speed or accuracy, and performance variations across denominations did not skew the total scores. The result is a balanced snapshot of the performance for each currency design.

The averages of accuracy and speed discussed in the narratives of Sections 6.3.1 through 6.3.7 represent the summary results from the total participants for all trials of each currency type, as shown in Figures 6-51 and 6-53 in Section 6.5. The figures in Section 6.3.1 through 6.3.7 (Figures 6-15 through 6-40) represent the average results per trial: a calculation to average these average data points may not yield the exact same results as Figures 6-51 and 6-53.

6.3.1. U.S. Dollar

U.S. dollars are the same size for all denominations (155 x 66 mm). There are large portraits, which vary by denomination, on the front of each note. The $5, $10, $20, and $50 notes issued since 1997 have large, high-contrast numerals at the lower-right corner on the back of the note. A machine-readable feature to facilitate development of handheld scanning devices for the blind and VI has been included in all redesigned notes issued since 1997. Redesigned notes issued since 2003 have a subtle background color, which also varies by denomination.

6.3.1.1. U.S. Dollar - VI Results

Figures 6-15 and 6-16 show the average recognition speed and accuracy scores, respectively, for VI participants for the newer (with background color) and older (without background color) U.S. denominations. The U.S. $5 note with background color also includes the large purple numeral 5.

Because visual impairments vary greatly and some notes are easier to denominate than others (e.g., the $100 notes take the longest), VI people use a variety of strategies to identify denominations. As shown in Figure 6-16, VI participants could identify, on average, both the notes with no background color and the later generation notes with background color a minimum average of 94% of the time.

VI participants indicated that they often identify objects based on blurry light/dark patterns. In these instances, the light/dark silhouette of each denomination was a valuable affordance, in some cases as important as the numeral size. For example, participants found that the relatively strong foreground/background color contrast of U.S. currency aids recognition. Based on this attribute, $1 notes were frequently recognized by their light-on-dark numbers and the large amount of nearly-solid ink on the back of the note.

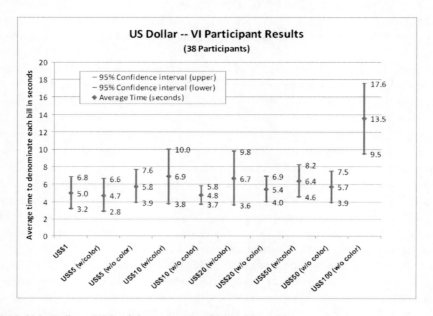

Figure 6-15. U.S. Dollar – VI Participant Average Times (seconds).

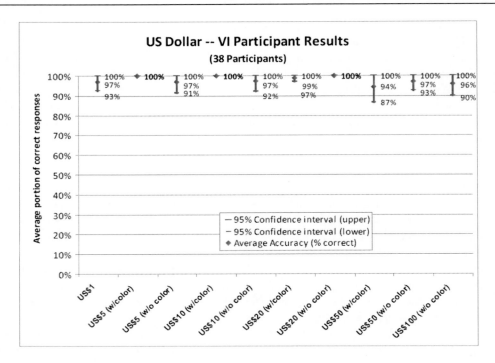

Figure 6-16. U.S. Dollar - VI Partficipant Accuracy.

Most VI participants indicated that the large purple numeral on the redesigned $5 note was helpful in the usability test. This was supported by the survey results (see Appendix D), where 56% of VI survey participants who responded to this question said that the new $5 note was easier to identify, although 10% said it was more difficult. Some VI participants said they would prefer a darker numeral, such as the green numeral used in the previous generation $5 note.

The test administrators observed that VI participants generally did not notice the background color on the front of the new $5 note, but two participants said that it slightly reduced the overall contrast. Two other participants said that the background color of the newer $20 note reduced the contrast noticeably. Figure 6-15 shows that, with the exception of the $5 note, VI participants found that denominating notes with the new background color was slower on average than with the older designs without the background color.

VI participants mentioned that $50 notes and $20 notes are easy to confuse because the large 5 and 2 numerals look similar. This effect was noted in currencies from other countries as well. The ARINC team observed that participants more easily confused the numerals 5 and 2 when the notes were compared upside down. This is a plausible scenario because participants often place the notes in their wallet upside down so that the large numeral at the bottom of the note is closer to the opening and easier to identify.

Participants said that they would prefer that the primary large numerals for denominating notes be located in the upper left or right corner, instead of the lower right corner. This change would place the large numeral, right-side up, nearer to the opening, enabling quicker denomination without removing the notes from a wallet. Similarly, VI participants said that they would prefer a large numeral on both sides so they could denominate a note without having to turn it over to find a particular feature.

The $100 note, which has not been redesigned for ten years, was the most difficult for VI participants to recognize, taking approximately twice as long for test participants to identify as other denominations. Several participants reported that, because the size and low contrast of the numerals make recognition difficult, $100 notes are most-often recognized by the silhouette on the front or by process of elimination (i.e., it isn't any of the other denominations). The denomination speed results (Figure 6-15) show the increased difficulty with this note compared to the other U.S. denominations, which, except for the $1 note, have been redesigned within the last ten years.

6.3.1.2. Conclusions – U.S. Dollar

- The VI participants could identify, on average, both the notes with no background color and the later generation notes with background color a minimum average of 94% of the time.
- The light/dark silhouette (portrait) of each denomination and strong foreground/background color contrast of U.S. currency aids recognition for VI participants.
- The large purple numeral on the redesigned $5 note was more helpful in the usability tests than the enlarged numerals on the $10, $20, and $50 notes.
- With the exception of the $5 note, VI participants found that denominating notes with the new background color was slower on average than with the older designs without background color.
- VI participants said that $50 notes and $20 notes are easy to confuse, because the 5 and 2 numerals look similar. This effect was noted with other currencies.
- VI participants said that they would prefer that the primary large numerals for denominating notes be located in the upper left corner, instead of the lower right corner, to enable quicker denomination without removing the notes from a wallet.
- VI participants took almost twice as long to identify the $100 note as they did to identify the other denominations.

6.3.2. United Kingdom Pound

UK pounds vary proportionally in size in two dimensions with denomination. The primary colors are different for each denomination. There are large-print numerals in the upper left corner of the front of each note (except the £50 note), and smaller high-contrast numerals in the upper right corner of the front of the note (except the newer £20 note). The backs of the notes have much lower contrast, without any large-print numerals. There is also a graphic geometric pattern on each note. The new £20 note does not include the graphic geometric pattern.

UK pounds include a foil patch on the £20 and £50 notes and a foil strip on the £10 and £5 notes. The location of the foil patch or strip, relative to the edges of the notes, is different for each denomination.

6.3.2.1. UK Pound - Blind Participant Results

Figures 6-17 and 6-18 show the average recognition times and average accuracy scores, respectively, for blind participant usability tests of UK pound denominations.

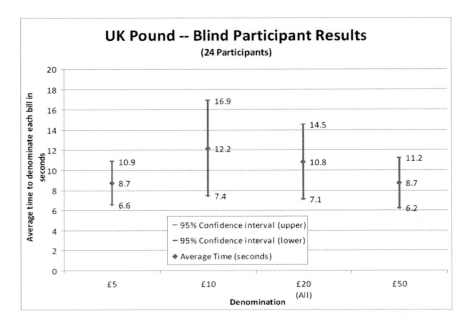

Figure 6-17. UK Pound - Blind Participant Average Times (seconds).

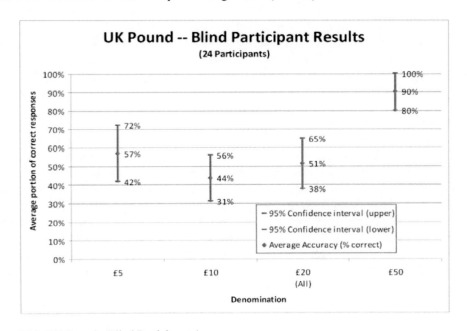

Figure 6-18. UK Pound - Blind Participant Accuracy.

Usability test results indicate that the largest (£50) and smallest (£5) notes had the highest accuracy denomination success rates (90% and 57%, respectively) for the blind participants. Test administrators noted that £20 notes were sometimes confused with the £50 notes and £10 notes were sometimes confused with £5 notes.

The test administrators observed that blind participants found it difficult to find the foil patches on the notes. Once they located the patches, blind participants found the foil patches difficult to differentiate. Participants found that a blank (little or no ink) area of the paper felt very similar in smoothness to an area covered by a foil patch or strip. On the newest (Series F) £20 note, the large blank area on the left side of the front of the note is exactly the location where the foil patches are located on the still-circulating Series E £5 and £10 notes.

6.3.2.2. UK Pound - VI Participant Results

Figures 6-19 and 6-20 show the average recognition times and average accuracy scores, respectively, for VI participant usability tests of UK pound denominations.

VI participants were able to identify UK pound denominations with an average accuracy of 90%. Three VI participants found that the large numerals on the newest (Series F) £20 notes were easier to identify than the thicker, but lower-contrast, numerals on the older Series E notes. Several VI participants found the smaller high-contrast numerals on the Series E notes to be easier to identify than the larger numerals on the same notes. The VI participants said they perceived the color formats used in UK pounds to be muted, such that it was easier for them to search for the numerals than to identify the base colors. As with the U.S. $100 note, the VI participants said the numerals on the £50 note were more difficult to see than on any of the other denominations. While this did not significantly affect VI participants' accuracy (Figure 6-20), it did increase the average time required for denomination (Figure 6-19) over the other denominations.

6.3.2.3. Conclusions – UK Pound

- The largest (£50) and smallest (£5) UK notes had highest accuracy denomination success rates for blind participants (90% and 57%, respectively).
- Blind participants found it difficult to find the foil patches on the notes. Once they located the patches, blind participants found the foil patches difficult to differentiate.
- VI participants were able to identify UK pound denominations with an average accuracy of 90%.
- The numerals on the £50 note were more difficult for VI participants to read than on the other denominations. While this did not significantly affect VI participants' accuracy (93%), it did increase the average time required for denomination. In general, VI participants use vision as the primary method to identify the notes, and resorted to estimating size differences only when they were unsure.

6.3.3. Euros

Like the UK pound, euros vary proportionally with denomination in size in two dimensions. Usability tests included the €5, €10, €20, €50, and €100 notes. The back of the euro note has a large-print numeral in the upper right corner, set above the artwork, and a smaller high-contrast numeral in the lower right corner. There is a high contrast, medium-size numeral in the lower right corner and a low contrast, medium-size numeral in the lower left corner (slightly larger and higher contrast for the €50 and €100) on the back. Base color differences between the denominations are quite dramatic. The silhouettes are fairly consistent across notes, although pattern differences are introduced with the changes in note sizes. The €5, €10, and €20 notes have a foil strip along the left side of the front. The €50 and €100 notes have foil patches on the right side of the front of the note. The foil patches were pointed out to participants to assess the feasibility of using them to differentiate a €20 note from a €50 note.

6.3.3.1. Euro - Blind Participant Results

Figures 6-21 and 6-22 show the average recognition times and average accuracy scores, respectively, for blind participant usability tests of euro denominations.

As shown in Figure 6-22, the blind participants were able to recognize the €5 note more accurately (average of 87%) than the other denominations (averages ranged from 51% to 57%). The test administrators noted that the €50 and €10 were frequently misidentified as €100 and €5 notes, respectively. Incorrect denominations were usually confused with notes closest in size, the next-higher or next-lower denomination.

The participant comments indicated that they attributed their error rates to the small differences in sizes between denominations. Many blind participants said that they believed they would be able to get used to the euro size format with more practice. Some blind participants reported that their experience was that their accuracy improved when they handled euro notes frequently while traveling. Other blind participants said that they always needed a reference object against which to compare the size of the notes.

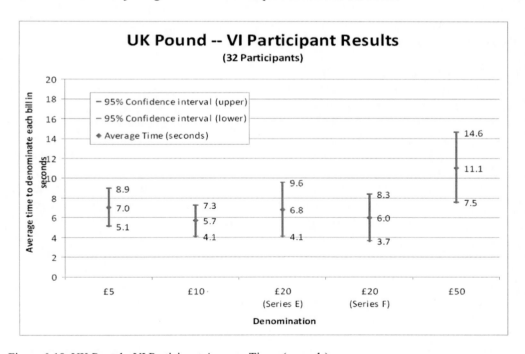

Figure 6-19. UK Pound - VI Participant Average Times (seconds).

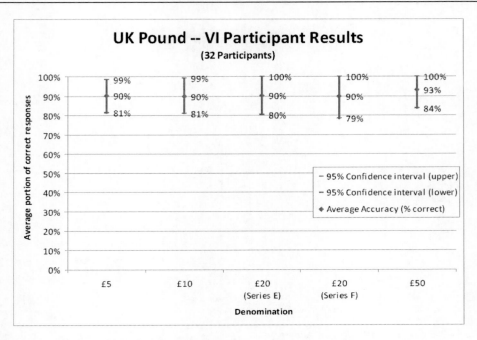

Figure 6-20. UK Pound - VI Participant Accuracy.

Blind participants attempted to use the foil strip to differentiate the €20 and €50 notes, but many could not locate the foil strips by touch.

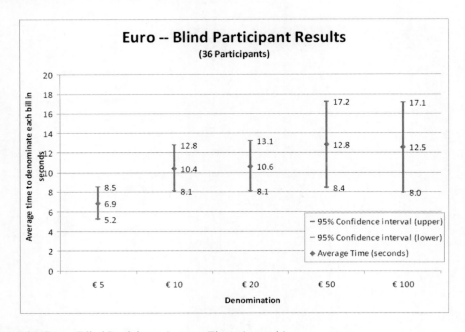

Figure 6-21. Euro - Blind Participant Average Times (seconds).

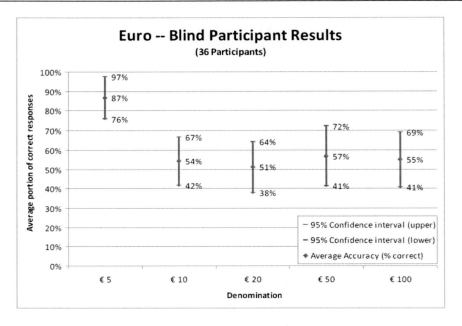

Figure 6-22. Euro - Blind Participant Accuracy.

6.3.3.2. Euro - VI Participant Results

Figures 6-23 and 6-24 show the average recognition times and average accuracy scores, respectively, for VI participant usability tests of euro denominations.

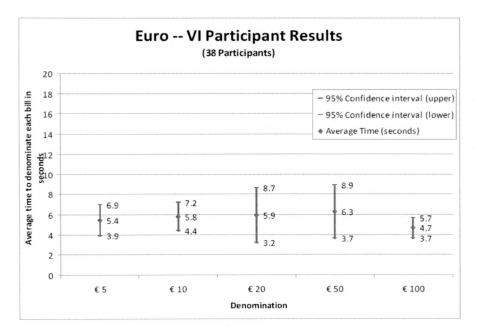

Figure 6-23. Euro - VI Participant Average Times (seconds).

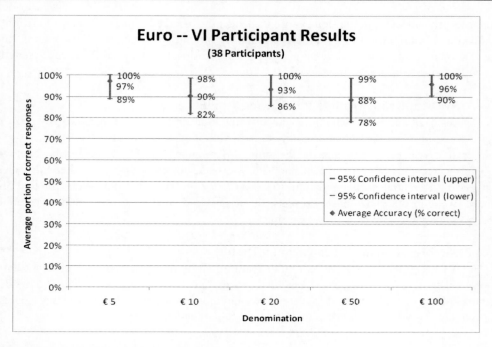

Figure 6-24. Euro - VI Participant Accuracy.

Usability tests indicate that VI people were able to denominate euros quickly, on average between 4.7 and 6.3 seconds and between 88% and 97% accuracy.

The test administrators noted the following subjective comments and observations:

- The primary large print numerals on the front of the note were easily visible.
- The €5 note was recognizable primarily by the small note size

6.3.3.3. Conclusions – Euro

- Blind participants recognized the €5 note more accurately than the other denominations (average of 87% vs. averages ranging from 51%–57%).
- Blind participants incorrectly denominated euros when they confused one denomination with the next-higher or next-lower denomination because it was hard for them to perceive the small size differences between denominations.
- VI people were able to denominate euros quickly (4.7–6.3 seconds) and accurately (88%–97%).
- The primary large print numerals on the front of the note were easily visible for VI participants.
- The €5 note was recognizable primarily by the small note size.

6.3.4. Swedish Kronor

The usability testing included four Swedish kronor notes, the SEK20, SEK50, SEK100, and SEK500. Swedish kronor vary in color and size in two dimensions. For blind users, the size variance is the only feature useful for denomination. Unlike the euro and UK pound, kronor length and width dimensions vary independently. The 20 kronor is 120 mm × 67 mm; the 50 kronor is 120 mm × 77 mm; the 100 kronor is 140 mm × 72 mm; the 500 kronor is 150 mm × 82 mm. This non-proportional assignment of sizes enables larger differences in length and width between denominations.

6.3.4.1. Swedish Kronor - Blind Participant Results

Figures 6-25 and 6-26 show the average recognition times and average accuracy scores, respectively, for blind participant usability tests of kronor denominations.

For the Swedish notes, size is the only differentiator for blind users. The average recognition accuracy of between 52% and 91% was better for kronor than for other currencies using size differential accommodation, (51%–87% for the euro and 44%–90% for the UK pound). As with other size-based formats, the largest and smallest denominations were the most accurately recognized by blind participants.

6.3.4.2. Swedish Kronor - VI Participant Results

For VI users, the primary accessibility features of the Swedish notes are different base colors and large dark numbers on a lighter background in one upper corner of each side. Figures 6-27 and 6-28 show the average recognition times and average accuracy scores, respectively, for VI participant usability tests of kronor denominations.

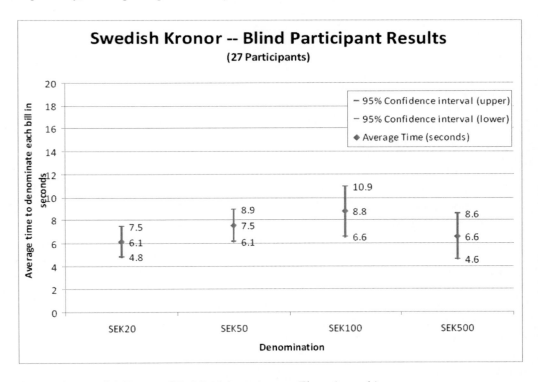

Figure 6-25. Swedish Kronor - Blind Participant Average Times (seconds).

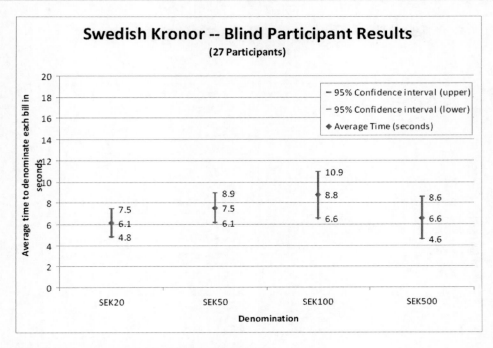

Figure 6-26. Swedish Kronor - Blind Participant Accuracy.

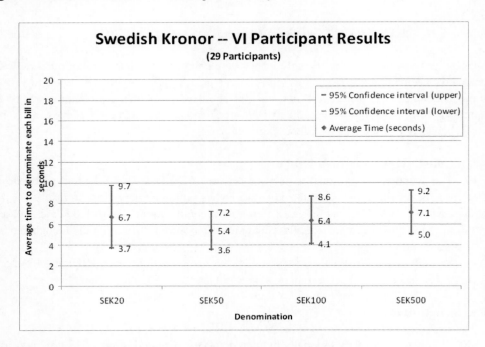

Figure 6-27. Swedish Kronor - VI Participant Average Times (seconds).

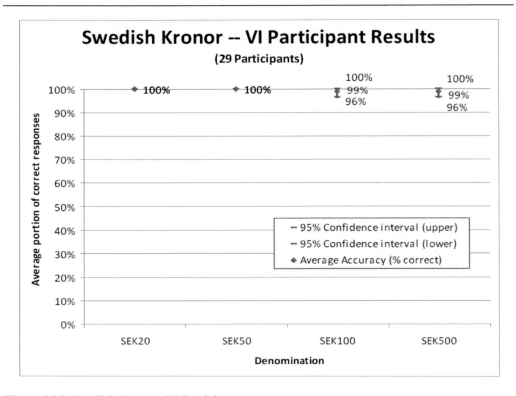

Figure 6-28. Swedish Kronor - VI Participant Accuracy.

Usability tests indicate that VI participants were able to denominate kronor quickly, with averages between 5.4 and 7.1 seconds, with an average accuracy ranging from 99% to 100%. Although the VI participants were not specific about what factors made kronor easier to denominate than other currencies, the ARINC team noted that these notes have a strong contrast between the numerals and the background.

6.3.4.3. Conclusions – Swedish Kronor
- The average recognition accuracy of between 52% and 91% for blind participants was better for kronor than for other currencies (although very close to results for the euro at 51% to 87%) using size differential accommodation. As with other size-based formats, the largest and smallest denominations were most accurately recognized by blind participants.
- VI participants were able to denominate kronor quickly (averages ranging from 5.4 to 7.1 seconds) and accurately (averages ranging from 99% to 100%).

6.3.5. Swiss Franc
The usability testing included three Swiss notes, the Swiss franc CHF10, CHF20, and CHF50. The Swiss notes vary in length, by increments of 11 mm (126 mm, 137 mm, and 148 mm). The width of all the notes is 74 mm.

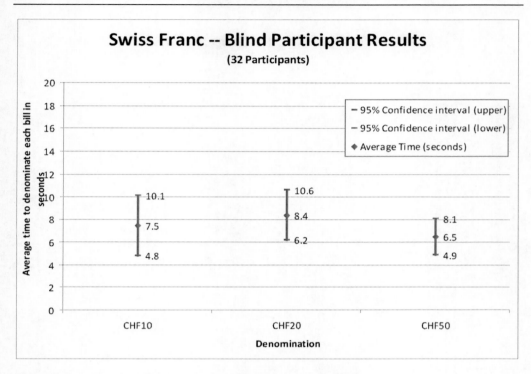

Figure 6-29. Swiss Franc - Blind Participant Average Times (seconds).

Swiss notes have starkly different base colors. The denomination numerals are in three places on the front of the note, and two places on the back. On the front, the larger numerals have low contrast with the background while the smaller numerals have very high contrast.

Swiss francs have an intaglio geometric tactile feature. None of the initial blind participants were able to discriminate between any of the symbols; they all found the note size differences much more reliable. Therefore, the ARINC team did not discuss the intaglio tactile feature for the remainder of the usability testing.

6.3.5.1. Swiss Franc - Blind Participant Results

Figures 6-29 and 6-30 show the average recognition times and average accuracy scores, respectively, for blind participant usability testing of Swiss franc denominations.

The timing results (Figure 6-29) show that blind participants were able to denominate Swiss francs, with length difference of 11 mm between denominations, on average within 6.5 to 8.4 seconds. This was much faster than with Australian notes (average of 11.3 to 15.4 seconds), which also only vary along one dimension, but with 7 mm length differences (see Figure 6-33 for Australian note results).

The accuracy results in Figure 6-30 show that blind participants were able to denominate Swiss francs, with accuracy scores averaging between 54% and 78%. This was a bit better than the 36% to 76% average denomination accuracy measured for Australian currency, which also had size changes along only one dimension (Figure 6-34).

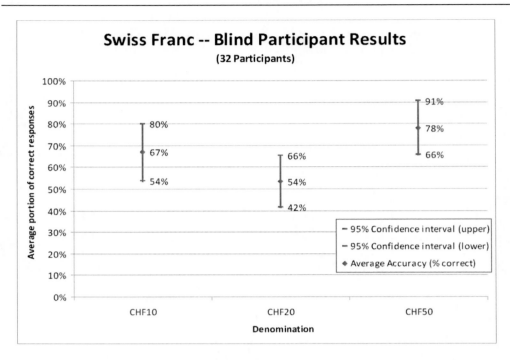

Figure 6-30. Swiss Franc - Blind Participant Accuracy.

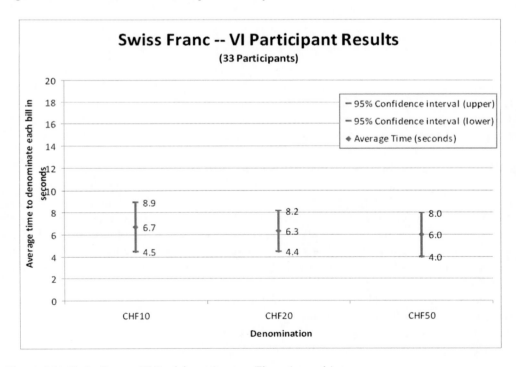

Figure 6-31. Swiss Franc - VI Participant Average Times (seconds).

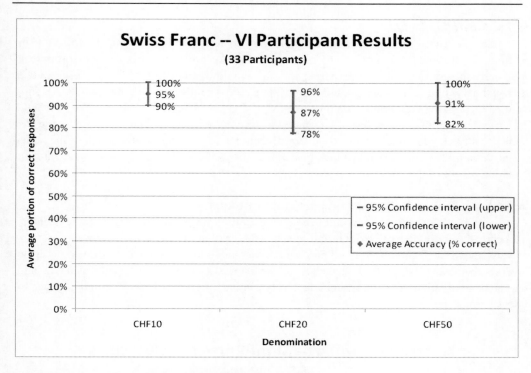

Figure 6-32. Swiss Franc - VI Participant Accuracy.

6.3.5.2. Swiss Franc - VI Participant Results

Figures 6-31 and 6-32 show the average recognition times and average accuracy scores, respectively, for VI participant usability tests of Swiss franc denominations.

Figure 6-32 shows that the test participants were able to correctly denominate the Swiss franc on average between 87% and 95% of the time. The average time to denominate (Figure 6-31) does not vary significantly by denomination. The test administrators observed that the VI participants most often relied on the numerals for denomination of the notes, rather than relying on the base color differences. VI participants who said they had reduced color vision noted that the large, medium-contrast numerals on the back of the notes were sufficient for denomination and that the base color variations were not as useful.

6.3.5.3. Conclusions – Swiss Franc

- Blind participants were able to denominate Swiss francs, with length difference, with accuracy scores averaging between 54% and 78%.
- VI participants most often relied on the numerals for denomination of the notes, rather than relying on the base color differences.
- VI test participants were able to correctly denominate the Swiss franc on average between 87% and 95% of the time, with minimal differences between the denominations.

6.3.6. Australian Dollar

Like the Swiss francs, Australian dollars vary in length only (130 mm to 158 mm, in increments of 7 mm. All notes are 65 mm wide). The Australian notes have a polypropylene polymer substrate, with a transparent plastic window embedded in one corner. The transparent windows are over-printed with white patterns, and some (i.e., the AU$20, AU$50, and AU$100) are over- struck with numerals.

Each Australian note has its own color format, with each denomination having a consistent base color that is distinctly different from the other denominations. All of the notes have large-print numerals indicating their value, using the same size, pattern, and relative position on both sides of the note.

6.3.6.1. Australian Dollar - Blind Participant Results

Figures 6-33 and 6-34 show the average recognition times and average accuracy scores, respectively, for blind participant usability tests of Australian dollar denominations.

As shown in Figure 6-33, blind participants were able to denominate Australian notes on average between 11.3 to 15.4 seconds. For the AU$20 (where there are both smaller and larger denomination sizes that might feel very similar) participants took slightly longer to identify the denomination.

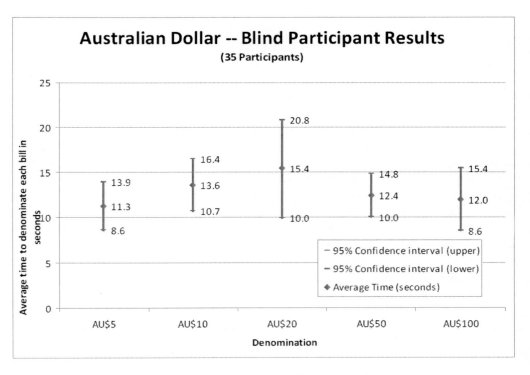

Figure 6-33. Australian Dollar - Blind Participant Average Times (seconds).

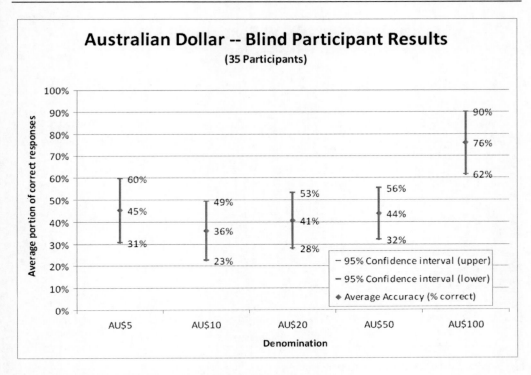

Figure 6-34. Australian Dollar - Blind Participant Accuracy.

The results show that, as with the notes that vary in size in both dimensions, the largest (AU$100) and smallest (AU$5) values for the Australian dollars were most reliably denominated by the blind participants. This was especially true for the largest AU$100 notes, which were correctly identified 76% of the time by blind participants (see Figure 6-34). The test administrators noted that, as with the EU and UK currencies, the AU$50 and AU$10 denominations were frequently mistaken for the AU$5 and AU$100 denominations, respectively.

The test administrators observed that a few blind participants found the plastic window inserts on the notes useful in determining denomination.

6.3.6.2. Australian Dollar - VI Participant Results

Figures 6-35 and 6-36 show the average recognition times and average accuracy scores, respectively, for VI participant usability tests of Australian dollar denominations.

The test results show that VI participants were able to consistently denominate all Australian dollar denominations quickly (averaging less than 6.2 seconds) and accurately (averaging 98%–100%). The test participants indicated that the stark base color differences and the size and clarity of the type used for the numerals were both useful in denomination.

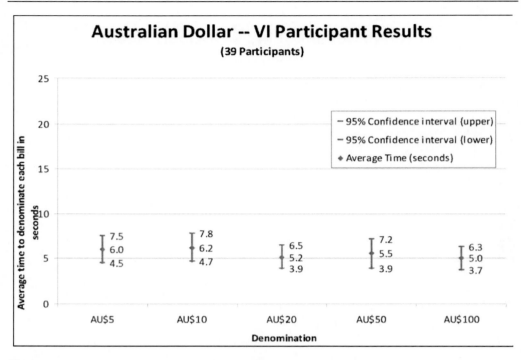

Figure 6-35. Australian Dollar - VI Participant Average Times (seconds).

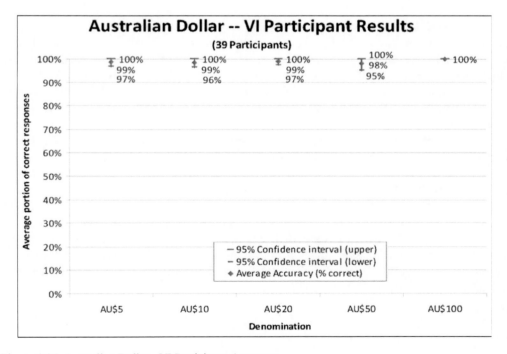

Figure 6-36. Australian Dollar - VI Participant Accuracy.

6.3.6.3. Conclusions – Australian Dollar
- Blind participants were able to denominate Australian notes (7 mm length increments) less accurately than Swiss notes (11 mm length increments).
- The stark base color differences and the size and clarity of the type used for the numerals helped VI participants denominate Australian notes quickly (less than 6.2 seconds on average) and accurately (averaging 98–100%).

6.3.7. Canadian Dollar

Canadian dollars are the same size for each denomination, and each has a different base color, but with similarly shaped design patterns. Each Canadian note includes a tactile feature consisting of a pattern of clustered raised dots. These 6-dot clusters are similar in size and appearance to a Braille cell, but with all dots raised. The number of clusters of these cells indicate the value of the notes–one cluster of six dots for a CA$5 note, two clusters for a CA$10 note, three clusters for a CA$20 note, four clusters for a CA$50 note, and two clusters, split with a space in between them for the CA$100 note.

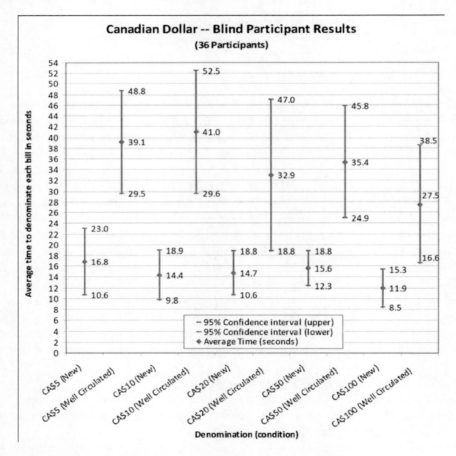

Figure 6-37. Canadian Dollar - Blind Participant Average Times (seconds).

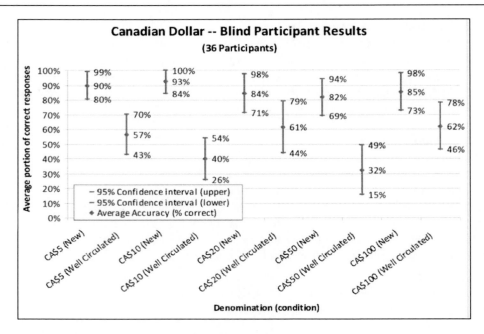

Figure 6-38. Canadian Dollar - Blind Participant Accuracy.

The height of the dots (140 microns) is less than traditional Braille (400 microns), but published research[32] has demonstrated that the clusters are easily detectable when the note is new. However, the dots are flattened as notes circulate and experience wear. Substantiating the ability of the blind to detect the dots on widely circulated notes was one of the objectives of this usability test. Therefore, some of the sample notes used in the study were new and some were widely circulated. The ARINC team did not have a method to clearly measure the extent of wear and tear on the widely circulated notes, but the test participants said they could easily tell the difference between widely circulated and new notes by feel.

Recently issued Canadian notes include a foil strip along the left side of the note, running width- wise under the small-print numerals. Canadian notes also include large-print numerals, printed with particularly heavy intaglio ink, with high foreground/background contrast. The numerals are set into a colored background of the note, but a very light "halo" border surrounding the numerals provides contrast. The numerals in recent-generation notes include a speckled pattern with relatively thick lines. Older notes included slightly thinner, solid lines (these older notes did not have foil strips). Two of the older CA$5 notes were included in the sample set to assess the relative effectiveness of the two types of design features.

6.3.7.1. Canadian Dollar - Blind Participant Results

Figures 6-37 and 6-38 show the average recognition times and average accuracy scores, respectively, for blind participant usability tests of Canadian dollar denominations, in both new and widely circulated condition.

Blind participants were able to denominate new Canadian notes fairly accurately as shown in Figure 6-38 (on average between 82% and 93%). However, recognition accuracy for widely circulated notes was reduced to between 32% and 62%, depending on the denomination. Figure 6-37 indicates that the time required to identify denominations was relatively high, with an average time between 11.9 and 16.8 seconds for new notes, and between 27.5 and 41 seconds for widely circulated notes. The test administrators observed that the long recognition times were due primarily to difficulty in locating the raised dots. Some blind participants were able to use the foil security strip to orient the note to more-easily locate the raised dots, but others could not locate the foil strips.

6.3.7.2. Canadian Dollar - VI Participant Results

Figures 6-39 and 6-40 show the average recognition times and average accuracy scores, respectively, for VI participant usability tests of Canadian dollar denominations, in both new and widely circulated condition. The results are not broken out for new vs. widely circulated because VI participants noted they did not rely on the raised dots to denominate this currency.

The results of the usability tests indicate that VI participants were able to denominate Canadian notes quickly (within an average of 4.4 to 6.5 seconds for all denominations) and accurately (average at least 96% for all denominations). The VI participants indicated that they strongly appreciated the large-print numerals of the Canadian notes; that the size and foreground/background contrast levels were helpful, and that they preferred the thicker speckled print over the thinner solid print that was present in the older design of the CA$5 notes.

The test administrators noted the following subjective comments made by VI test participants:

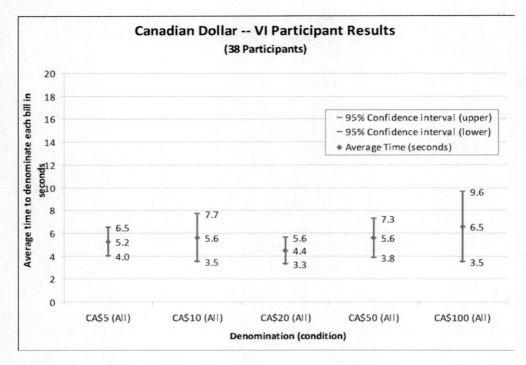

Figure 6-39. Canadian Dollar - VI Participant Average Times (seconds).

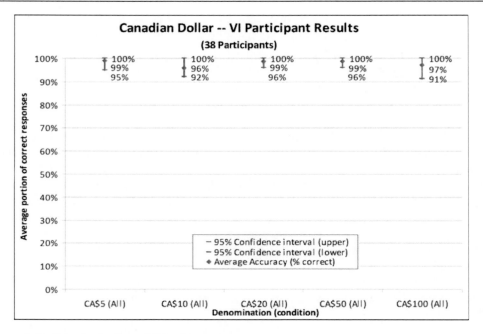

Figure 6-40. Canadian Dollars - VI Participant Accuracy.

- The color differences between denominations were helpful in identifying the notes.
- The interwoven security thread on the back of the notes interferes somewhat with the legibility of the light-on-dark numerals.

6.3.7.3. Conclusions – Canadian Dollar
- Blind participants were able to use the tactile feature, consisting of a pattern of clustered raised dots, to denominate new Canadian notes accurately, identifying between 82% and 93% of the notes correctly, depending on denomination.
- Recognition accuracy for widely circulated notes was reduced significantly (average between 32% and 62%, depending on denomination) for blind participants.
- The time required for blind participants to identify denominations was relatively high, due primarily to difficulty locating the tactile features.
- VI participants were able to denominate Canadian notes quickly (within an average of 4.4 to 6.5 seconds for all denominations) and accurately (average at least 96% for all denominations), primarily using the large-print numerals.

6.4. Usability Testing Results for Prototype Currency Accommodations

The ARINC team conducted usability testing of four developmental prototypes of potential currency accommodations with blind participants. The purpose of these tests was to establish the effectiveness of different features of the various currency designs. The prototype sets are illustrated in Appendix K.

The ARINC team tested four sets of sample currency accommodations. Two sets included cut paper samples (100% cotton resume paper) with different sizes representing each denomination, and size limitations in accordance with currency production and processing machinery physical limitations. One of these sets varied in length only and the other varied in both length and width. The third and fourth sets were created from regular U.S. currency paper, which is made from cotton and linen fibers. One of these sets had a system of notches cut along the top and bottom of the note with different patterns to represent each denomination. The other set had a system of heavy intaglio ink bars printed along the side margin of the notes.

Test results are reported in terms of recognition speed and recognition accuracy, with a 95% confidence interval, for each set of measurements. Average recognition speed was the measure of time beginning when the participant took the note in hand and ending when the participant declared the denomination. For the prototype currency features, each participant had up to twelve trials with each feature, with each denomination presented more than once.

Test analysts computed the average recognition accuracy for each participant, denomination, and currency accommodation. Each test participant was presented with each denomination multiple times within each test. Participants scored one for correct identification and zero for incorrect identification for each denomination. For example, if a participant examined a note three times and identified it correctly twice, the score would be 67% (2/3) accuracy.

The ARINC team averaged accuracy and speed results across all participants to ensure that the variable number of exposures, individual participant natural variation in speed or accuracy, and performance variations across sample denominations did not skew the total scores. The result is a balanced snapshot of the performance for each prototype currency design, equally weighted for each sample denomination.

The averages of accuracy and speed discussed in the narratives of Sections 6.4.1 through 6.4.4 represent the summary results from the total participants for all trials of each prototype currency. Because the figures in Section 6.4.1 through 6.4.4 (Figures 6-41 through 6-50) represent the average results per trial: a calculation to average these averages will not yield the same exact results as in the narratives.

6.4.1. One-Dimensional Sizes

The usability testing included a set of samples cut from 100% cotton, 24 pound resume-type paper that varied only in length (1-D). The ARINC team created these samples in accordance with the minimum size limitation of the length of existing U.S. currency and the maximum size length that can be accommodated by the currency printing and processing equipment planned for implementation by the BEP. All notes were the same width as current U.S. currency (i.e., 66 mm). Note lengths varied by 4 or 5 mm with each denomination—$1 = 156 mm, $5 = 161 mm, $10 = 166 mm, $20 = 171, $50 = 176 mm, and $100 = 180 mm. The samples included no printed features.

6.4.1.1. One-Dimensional Sizes - Blind Participants

The results of the usability tests, shown in Figures 6-41 and 6-42, indicate that blind participants had difficulty denominating the 1-D sample notes accurately. The average accuracy was just 41%. Participants responded quickly (average of nine seconds) with the 1-D sizes. However, some participants felt that additional time spent on identifying the note would not have improved their accuracy, and said that they had simply guessed. Figure 6-42 shows that over the twelve trials there was no significant improvement in accuracy.

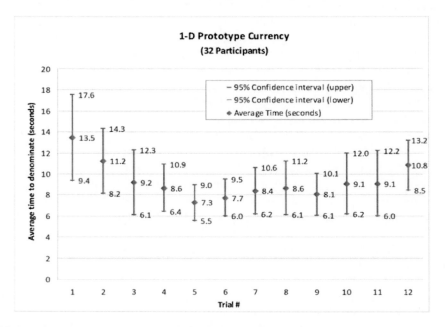

Figure 6-41. 1-D Prototype Currency - Blind Participant Average Time (seconds).

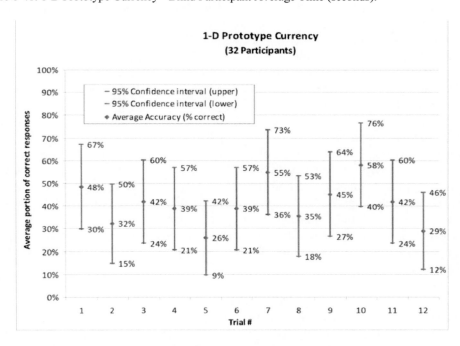

Figure 6-42. 1-D Prototype Currency - Blind Participant Average Accuracy.

The test administrators noted the following subjective comments made by blind test participants:

- Having a measuring device might make this system more useful, but even then the system would not be useful for verifying change while in line.
- The largest sized notes were too large to be practical.
- The participants said they did not feel that this system would be very helpful, even with practice.

6.4.1.2. Conclusions – 1-D Sizes

The 1-D size samples offered little benefit to blind users because the size differences between denominations were 5 mm or less.

6.4.2. Two-Dimensional Sizes

The usability testing included a set of samples cut from 100% cotton, 24 pound resume-type paper that varied both in length and width (2-D). The ARINC team created these samples in accordance with the minimum size limitation of the length and width of existing U.S. currency and the maximum size length and width that can be accommodated by the currency printing and processing equipment planned for implementation by the BEP. Notes varied in length and width using a system with three lengths and two widths, for six different sizes. Note length and width varied with denomination — $1 = 156 mm x 66 mm, $5 = 156 mm x 82 mm, $10 = 168 mm x 66 mm, $20 = 168 mm x 82 mm, $50 = 180 mm x 66 mm, and $100 = 180 mm x 82 mm. The samples included no printed features.

6.4.2.1. Two-Dimensional Sizes - Blind Participants

The results of the usability tests, shown in Figures 6-43 and 6-44, indicate that blind participants were better at denominating the 2-D sizes than the 1-D sizes, but still had trouble with accurate identification. The average accuracy was 63%, even after practice. Participants responded slightly slower with the 2-D sizes than with the 1-D sizes (average speed 10.7 seconds vs. nine seconds for 1-D). Some of the participants noted that they were more confident that they could figure out the denomination if they kept trying. The test administrators observed that discriminating between the different lengths was more difficult for the participants than discriminating between different widths. Figure 6-44 shows that there was no significant improvement in accuracy over the twelve trials. The test administrators noted that some errors throughout the test were attributable to the participants forgetting the denomination assignment pattern, rather than incorrectly identifying the shape of the notes. Learning the system took an average of 295 seconds. The test administrators observed that some of the older participants had difficulty remembering the denomination assignment pattern.

The test administrators noted the following subjective comments made by blind test participants:

- The participants had mixed opinions on the efficacy of the 2-D sizes, i.e., some felt that this system would be very helpful after some practice, while others did not.

- There was also a range of opinions among participants about the ease of use of the denomination pattern that the ARINC team used in testing. Some participants said that the denomination assignment pattern was simple and easy to remember. Others said that the denomination assignment pattern was potentially too difficult; even though they thought they could remember the values and adjust to the system over time.
- The participants said that the largest-sized notes were too large to be practical.

6.4.2.2. Conclusions – 2-D Sizes

- The 2-D size change system could work for some users, but appears to be ineffective for a substantial portion of participants.
- Test participants considered the largest 2-D note size to be impractically large.

6.4.3. Notches

The BEP created the notched sample set using regular U.S. currency paper cut to the same size as existing U.S. currency. The denomination of each note was determined by the number and location of small notches that were cut from the long edge (top and bottom) of each note. The notches were placed in three standard locations on each side of the note (see Appendix K for illustration). The notches along the top were mirrored on the bottom of the note, so participants only had to check one side of each note.

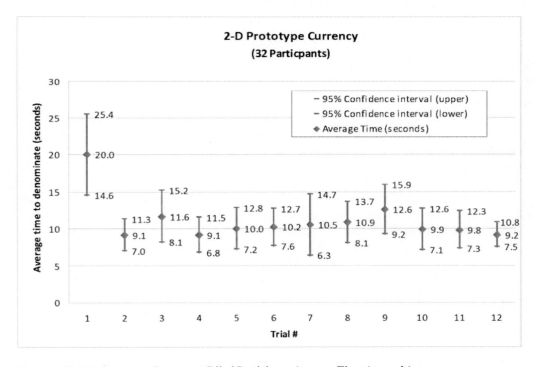

Figure 6-43. 2-D Prototype Currency - Blind Participant Average Time (seconds).

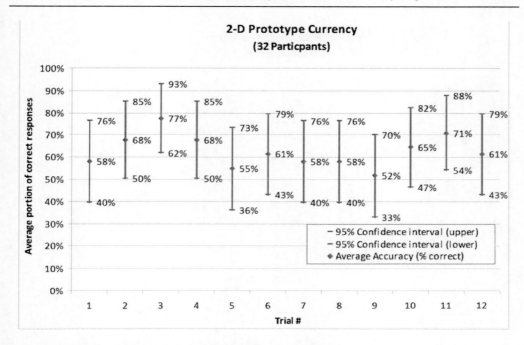

Figure 6-44. 2-D Prototype Currency - Blind Participant Average Accuracy.

With this sample set, participants were asked to remember the denomination patterns and use them correctly to identify the sample notes. Participants took an average of 280 seconds to learn the system. Three potential participants, all over age 70, decided during training that they did not like the notch system and discontinued testing.

6.4.3.1. Notches - Blind Participant Results

The results of the usability tests, shown in Figures 6-45 and 6-46, indicate that blind participants were better at denominating the notches than either of the size sample notes. Most blind participants were able to denominate the system of notches accurately (average of 89%) and quickly. The test administrators observed that some of the errors were attributable to participants forgetting the denomination assignment pattern and some were related to not correctly identifying the number of notches that were present. Most participants found the encoding system easy to learn, the average speed was 8.5 seconds. The test administrators observed that the notch spacing system appeared to be sufficiently detectable with practice, although some participants had some initial difficulty with it.

The test administrators noted the following subjective comments made by blind test participants:

- The denomination assignment pattern was easier to remember than the 2-D size system.
- The denomination assignment pattern was potentially too difficult; even though the participants thought they could remember the values and adjust to the system over time.

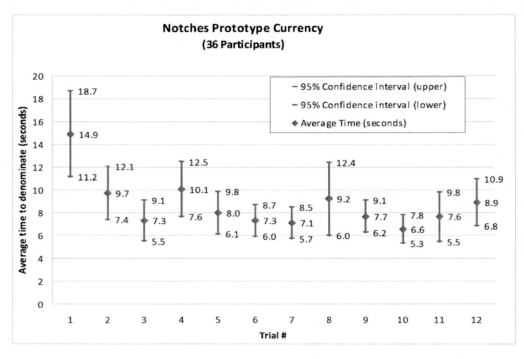

Figure 6-45. Notches Prototype Currency - Blind Participant Average Time (seconds).

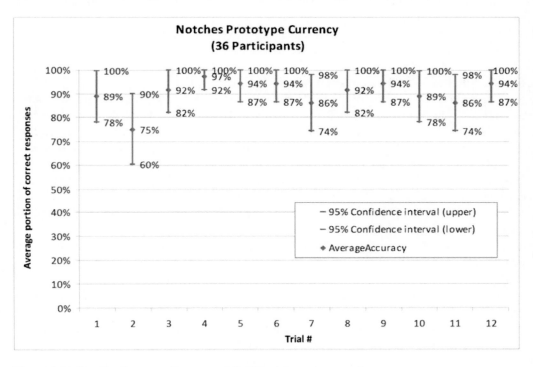

Figure 6-46. Notches Prototype Currency - Blind Participant Average Accuracy.

6.4.3.2. Conclusions – Notches

- Unlike every other method tested, the notch system was easy enough to use for most participants in all usage scenarios. Most participants said they would use this method to confirm the denomination of change they receive in transactions, even while in line with people waiting behind them.
- For some participants, the notch system was too difficult to remember.

6.4.4. Intaglio Printed Bars

The BEP created the intaglio-printed bar samples on regular U.S. currency paper. The prototype was a series of bars printed with heavy intaglio ink in the margin of each sample note. Each note included clusters of five bars, each bar approximately 1 mm wide, 4 mm long, and 2 mm apart, printed on one short edge of the note in the normally blank margin (see Appendix K for illustration). The pattern of bars on one side was mirrored on the other side of the note, so participants only had to check one side of each note. All notes were the same size as existing U.S. currency. Because there were only three patterns of bars in this sample, participants were not asked to remember which pattern was associated with a particular denomination, rather, they were asked only to identify the number of patches of bars (i.e., zero, one, two, or three).

6.4.4.1. Intaglio Printed Bars - Blind Participant Results

Performance on this prototype set varied greatly between participants. Figures 6-47 and 6-48 show the results for the newly printed bar feature. Overall, the accuracy for the newly printed bar features was good and the recognition speed was similar to the value measured for the newly printed Canadian tactile feature. The average accuracy was 85% for newly printed features, which is similar to the value measured for the notched sample set. However, the average speed of approximately 17.1 seconds was slower than the value measured for the notched sample set. The participants who reported themselves as being proficient in reading Braille were more likely to detect the presence of the bars accurately, but errors were still common.

The test administrators noted the following subjective comments made by blind test participants:

- Participants said they would require a flat surface to use this method, making it impractical in some usage scenarios.
- This method was not effective when the notes were simulated to be well circulated.

Figures 6-49 and 6-50 show the results for the notes that had simulated circulation via the normal BEP wear-simulating protocol. Both accuracy and speed were poor for the simulated well circulated notes. The average accuracy for simulated well circulated notes was significantly reduced (average of 42%) and the average speed for denomination took slightly longer (average of 20.6 seconds), as participants spent time trying to find the feature. Some of the participants declined to test these samples due to the difficulty identifying the bars during the training time.

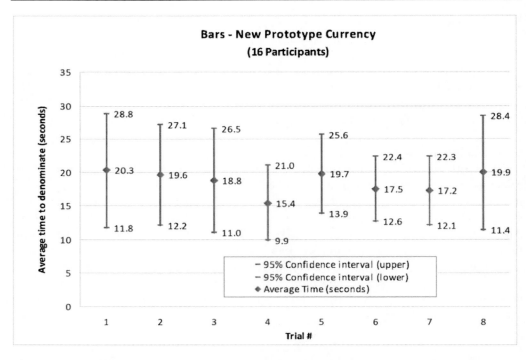

Figure 6-47. Bars (New) Prototype Currency - Blind Participant Average Time (seconds).

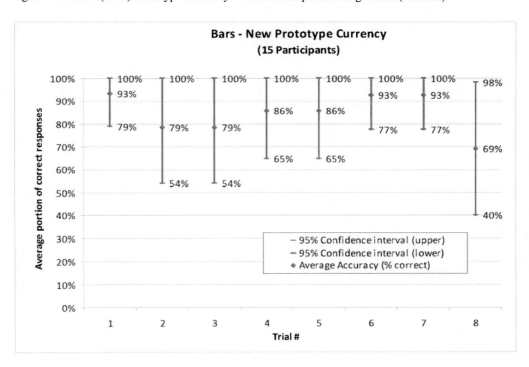

Figure 6-48. Bars (New) Prototype Currency - Blind Participant Average Accuracy.

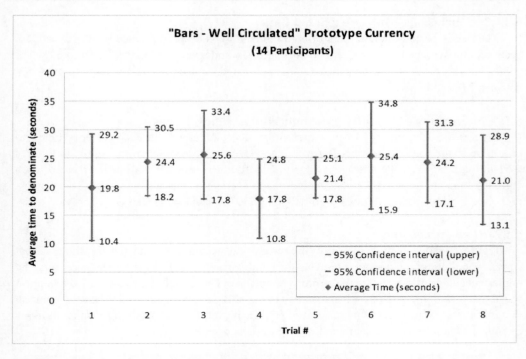

Figure 6-49. Bars (Well Circulated) Prototype Currency - Blind Participant Average Time (seconds).

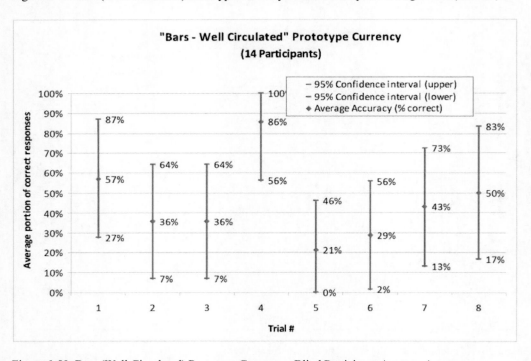

Figure 6-50. Bars (Well Circulated) Prototype Currency - Blind Participant Average Accuracy.

6.4.4.2. Conclusions – Intaglio Printed Bars

The newly printed intaglio bars offered moderately good performance both in speed and accuracy (on average between 15.4 and 20.3 seconds, and average accuracy between 69% and 93%), but the results were degraded for the simulated well circulated samples to accuracy between 21% and 86%.

6.5. Conclusions - Usability Testing (All Currency Types)

Figures 6-51 through 6-54 below present results summarized for each currency type and prototype in the usability testing. Because the average accuracy and speed results in Figures 6-51 through 6-54 are the averages of the total participant results for all of the trials of each currency type and prototype, a calculation of the average of the averages on the data points presented in Figures 6-15 through 6-50 will not yield the exact same results.

6.5.1. Blind Participants

Figures 6-51 through 6-54 show the speed and accuracy results for the international currency and prototype currency samples for blind participants. The participants achieved the highest accuracy results with the prototype notches. The Swedish kronor had the highest speed result but only at an average accuracy of 73%. Figures 6-52 and 6-54 show that among the prototype features, the blind test participants achieved the best usability results, in terms of both speed and accuracy combined, with the notched samples.

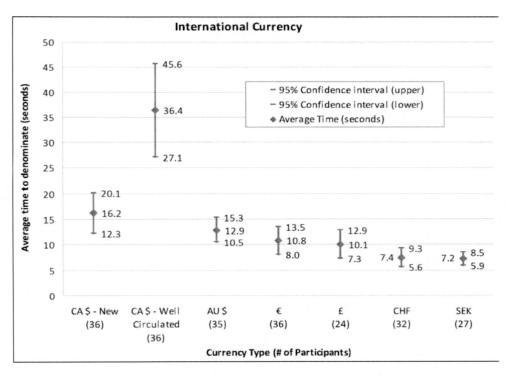

Figure 6-51. International Currency - Blind Participant Average Times (seconds).

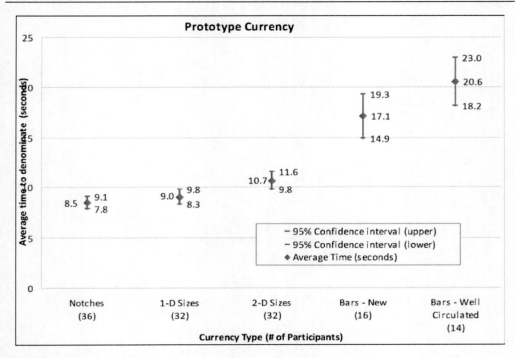

Figure 6-52. Prototype Currency - Blind Participant Average Times (seconds).

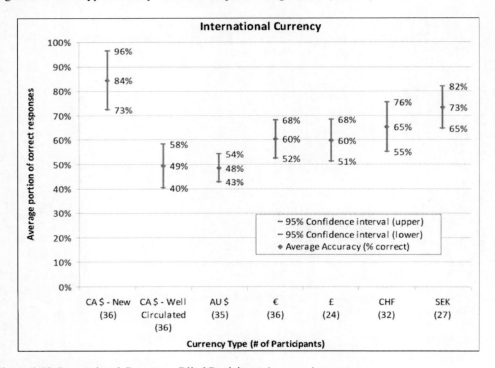

Figure 6-53. International Currency - Blind Participant Average Accuracy.

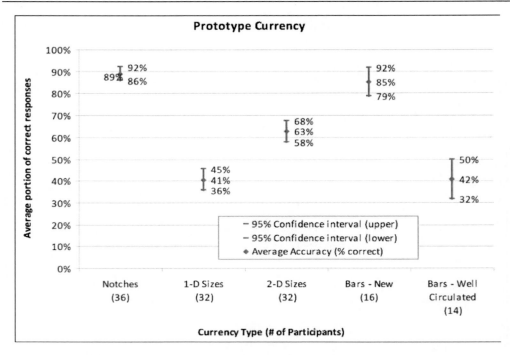

Figure 6-54. Prototype Currency - Blind Participant Average Accuracy.

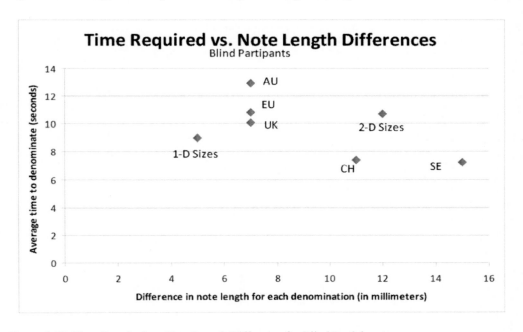

Figure 6-55. Time Required vs. Note Length Difference for Blind Participants.

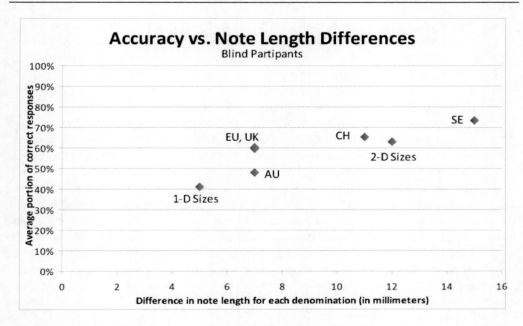

Figure 6-56. Average Accuracy vs. Note Length Difference for Blind Participants.

Figures 6-55 and 6-56 show the average time required for blind participants to denominate, and denomination accuracy, respectively, as a function of note length difference. Blind usability study participants were able to identify currency denominations more quickly and accurately when working with currency having irregular size differences between denominations (i.e., Swedish kronor) than with the currencies using proportional size differences (i.e., Australian dollar and euro).

The ARINC team developed the following conclusions from the blind participant usability tests:

- The notched prototype currency resulted in the highest accuracy score (89%) for blind participants.
- Blind participants were able to denominate the notched prototype currency nearly as quickly as the easiest international currencies with size differences (8.5 seconds for notches vs. 7.4 seconds for Swiss francs and 7.2 seconds for Swedish kronor).
- Test participants cited speed and ease of detecting the denomination as the most important factors in their measure of effectiveness of a currency feature. The notches and the easier size-based systems met the expectations of the participants for ease of use in the most difficult "receiving change" scenario.
- Raised dot tactile features, evaluated in tests of new Canadian notes, resulted in the second-highest accuracy score average of 84% for blind usability test participants. However, the time required for blind participants to identify denominations was relatively high, due primarily to difficulty locating the tactile features.

- Raised dot tactile features, evaluated in tests of widely circulated Canadian notes, resulted in accuracy scores reduced to an average of 49%. Ease of use in transaction scenarios would therefore decrease as the features experience wear from circulation.
- Currencies with the most distinct note size differences (Swiss francs and Swedish kronor) resulted in the quickest denomination performance for blind usability test participants. Smaller size differences (e.g., UK pound, euro, and Australian dollar), resulted in slower denomination. The 1-D sizes had the smallest size differences but were denominated fairly quickly in usability tests, primarily because participants were unsure about the denominations and, in many cases, told the test administrators that they were simply guessing.
- Test participants cited portability and speed of use as the most important factors in their willingness to use a reader device. The key factors described by participants were ease of carrying the device, speed of use, and social pressure to move along quickly. The smallest devices tested (Slide-in #2, Slide-in #3, and the cell phone #1) were considered by some participants to be portable enough that they would take the device with them when going shopping. However, few participants considered any of the devices fast enough to use to verify change while standing in line, saying they would step aside or wait until they were in a suitable location.
- Training and familiarity are important for both tactile and size affordances. The usability results are conservative because the participants encountered many different, but similar, systems in quick succession. In practice, there would be only one system in place and familiarization would likely improve results over time.

Figure 6-57. Average Time to Identify Currency for VI Participants.

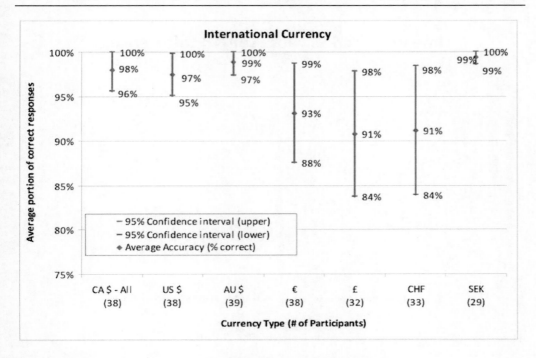

Figure 6-58. Average Accuracy of Currency Denomination for VI Participants.

6.5.2. VI Participants

Figures 6-57 and 6-58 show the usability testing results for the U.S. and international currencies, summarized by currency type, for VI participants. For these participants, the Canadian dollar and Australian dollar were both the fastest and the most accurate to denominate in usability tests. The euro had similar speed results, but was less accurate (average of 93% for euro, versus 98% for Canadian and 99% for Australian).

Figures 6-59 and 6-60 show the average time required for VI participants to denominate, and denomination accuracy, respectively, as a function of note length difference. The results do not show a significant relationship between size length differences and speed or accuracy of denomination for the VI participants. As was discussed in previous sections, although note size differences can be beneficial, the VI participants were more likely to use visual features (e.g., clarity of the primary numerals and the differences in base colors) to identify denomination. VI participants responded fairly quickly to the euro and Canadian and Australian dollars, which were also highly accurate; whereas the euro had a lower average accuracy.

The ARINC team developed the following conclusions from the VI participant usability tests:

- Over all trials, VI usability test participants were able to denominate the U.S. and international currencies tested with average accuracy ranging from 91% to 99%.
- Currency with large, high-contrast numerals (e.g., from the U.S., Canada, Australia, and Sweden) resulted in denomination accuracy rates above 95%.

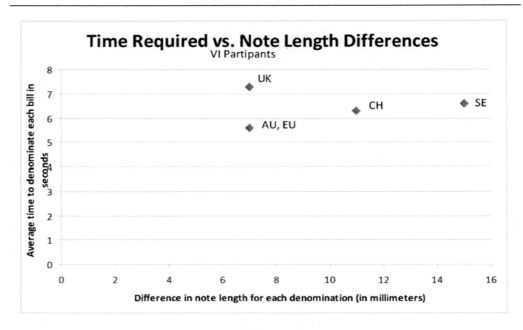

Figure 6-59. Time Required vs. Note Length Difference for VI Participants.

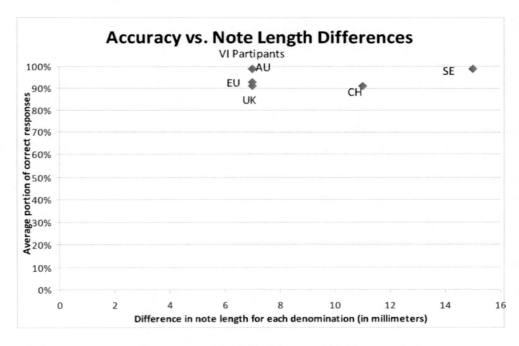

Figure 6-60. Average Accuracy vs. Note Length Difference for VI Participants.

Subtle background color differences like those used in the newer U.S. notes were not useful for VI participants. With the exception of the $5 note, VI participants found that denominating notes with the new background color was slower on average than with the older designs without the background color.

7. ECONOMIC ANALYSIS OVERVIEW

Based on the results of the analysis described in Sections 5 and 6, the BEP identified seven categories of accommodations for inclusion in the economic analysis. Upon further investigation of the accommodations, and based on results of the usability testing, the ARINC team, together with the BEP, selected an example accommodation within each category for further study. The cost analysis for each example was intended to establish a relevant scope and magnitude of the impact of each accommodation to provide a basis for comparison with the other alternatives. The economic analysis considered the costs as well as the qualitative benefits of each accommodation. The categories are as follows:

- Size changes along one dimension (length only, 1-D)
- Size changes along two dimensions (length and width, 2-D)
- Mechanical tactile features (notches or perforations)
- Raised tactile features (dots or bars)
- Embedded tactile features (strip or patch)
- Overt machine-readable features (readable by device)
- Currency reader devices

The costs and benefits of the accommodations that were considered included operational and technical impacts; cost to businesses, vendors, banks, and other handlers of currency; and benefits to the blind and VI community in the key usage scenarios described in Section 3.

The ARINC team used the following ground rules and assumptions for the economic analysis:

- Changes to the $1 and $2 notes were not considered for any of the accommodations.
    - The Omnibus Appropriations Act of 2009 states that none of the funds appropriated in this Act or otherwise available to the Department of the Treasury or the BEP may be used to redesign the $1 Federal Reserve note.
    - The $2 note is seldom used in day-to-day transactions.
- This study focused on accommodations for existing currency; therefore, replacing any denomination with a coin was not considered.
- Cost estimates for each of the accommodations were based on data available during the time period of the cost data gathering phase of this study (January 2009 through April 2009).
- Costs were based on rough order of magnitude (ROM) estimates by source data organizations and are appropriate for relative comparison of accommodations, but are not intended for budgetary purposes.

- Costs in this study are shown in constant fiscal year (FY) 2009 dollars. This removes the effect of inflation and allows relevant comparisons across alternatives.
- Analysis of benefits to the blind and VI community were based on results of the usability testing, surveys, and additional research conducted during this study.
- Any replacement of existing currency with new design currency would occur on a normal attrition basis; there will not be a one-time rollover/replacement. Multiple versions of each denomination will continue to circulate until the attrition process is complete.
- BEP printing operations will be based on a new larger sheet size format. Equipment necessary to process the larger sheet size is being developed. For purposes of this study, it is assumed that this equipment is already operational at BEP. It is estimated that this equipment replacement will take a minimum of three years.

This section includes a description of the methods and approach for the economic analysis, including the cost analysis (Section 7.1) and the benefits analysis (Section 7.2).

7.1. Cost Analysis Methodology

The ARINC team determined the estimated cost impact for each accommodation. Cost analysis results include initial nonrecurring (one-time) costs and annual recurring costs associated with each accommodation. The team considered three top-level categories of cost impacts in this study:

- U.S. Government, including the BEP, FRB, and the U.S. Secret Service
- U.S. market sectors, including commercial banking, automated teller machines (ATMs), vending, transportation, gaming, and retail equipment
- U.S. individuals, primarily the cost for reader devices

The ARINC team included relevant costs that could be gathered during the study time period. Although these data are representative of the scale and scope of the accommodations, there may be other market sectors, equipment manufacturers, etc., that would be affected by currency accommodations across the entire U.S. marketplace. The overall results of this study (i.e. the magnitude of the cost impact, and thus the feasibility of each accommodation) are not expected to change if additional information becomes available, unless a significant technological advance radically alters the considerations for a particular accommodation. Cost data are provided in Section 8.

7.1.1. U.S. Government

The ARINC team received cost inputs from three U.S. Government organizations: BEP, FRB, and the U.S. Secret Service. The cost data requested by the ARINC team included initial investment and nonrecurring costs, annual recurring costs, and lead times to implement the accommodations.

7.1.1.1. Bureau of Engraving and Printing

BEP personnel conducted an internal analysis of the impact of each currency accommodation on their manufacturing and operational processes. They considered the impact of each accommodation in terms of research and development, capital investment for new equipment and facilities, additional costs for existing equipment, note and ink design, testing, training, and public education. The BEP also identified recurring costs for labor and materials. The typical cycle for a new currency design is approximately seven to ten years; BEP estimated that the selected accommodations could be accomplished within that time frame.

The BEP currently prints all currency in a 32-subject per sheet format. The BEP plans to transition to a larger sheet size format to increase production capacity and to reduce labor and equipment costs. New production equipment is being acquired to enable the BEP to print the larger-sized sheets of currency. All features referenced in this study assume the BEP will be printing on larger size sheets by the time an accommodation is implemented.

The BEP estimates do not include specific costs resulting from decreased life span of notes associated with a currency feature, as durability testing has not been conducted on such accommodations. The BEP estimated that if a new feature reduced the durability of the notes, the shred rate would increase. At the point where widely circulated or defective notes increase the shred rate by about 25% per year (up to a total of 8.5 billion notes produced) on an ongoing basis, the BEP would need to invest in a third manufacturing facility. This facility would cost approximately $400 million, with annual operating expenses of $70 million. However, this is an upper bound, as it would only be required if a new feature decreased average note life span by more than one year.

7.1.1.2. Federal Reserve Bank

The Federal Reserve's CTO estimated the initial nonrecurring investment cost impact for the Federal Reserve System and the estimated impact on recurring costs of changes to note sizes. The CTO estimates included cost impacts associated with:

- Modifications to the high speed currency processing environment that the CTO manages on behalf of the Federal Reserve System's CPO and Reserve Banks.
- Changes in staffing levels for support provided to cash operations staff and management at the Reserve Banks.
- Training of the FRB cash operations management and staff.
- Decreased productivity from different sized notes.

The FRB estimates do not include specific costs resulting from decreased life span of notes associated with currency features. However, the FRB provided analogous information: an overall increase of 1% in the shred rate of the Series 2004 design notes was estimated to result in an incremental cost of $500,000 or more per denomination.[33]

7.1.1.3. United States Secret Service

The representative from the U.S. Secret Service estimated that there would be no additional cost to their organization for these accommodations, as the impact on their operations is on par with the impact of any normal currency design change. They indicated that there may be some additional training for size changes, which could be accommodated by the current workforce and would not require additional staff or materials. U.S. Secret Service costs are therefore not included in the economic analysis for each accommodation in Section 8.

7.1.2. U.S. Market Sectors

The ARINC team received cost inputs from U.S. market sectors, including banking and currency end-users (i.e., vending, retail, transportation, and gaming), as well as the top three (in terms of U.S. market share) Original Equipment Manufacturers (OEMs), who provided insight about national quantities of cash-handling machines across the market sectors. The ARINC team researched the costs associated with initial investment and nonrecurring costs, annual recurring costs, and lead times to implement the accommodations. For each of the market sectors that follow, the ARINC team obtained estimates from both the OEM and end user organizations (primarily national trade associations), and combined them to form an average estimated cost impact. The banking industry was the only market sector that estimated recurring costs after an initial investment. The OEMs and industry representatives for the other end-user sectors estimated that there would not be significant recurring costs after the initial investment and implementation of the accommodation. Therefore, the cost summaries in Section 8 only provide recurring costs for the U.S. Government and banking organizations. Although the impact of increased recurring costs for these organizations would be expected to diminish over time, the rate of change depends on the implementation strategy and schedule. For comparison between the accommodations, Section 8 provides estimated recurring costs for a one-year period after implementation.

7.1.2.1. High-Speed Machines

One of the OEMs for high-speed cash processing machines (that process currency in excess of 800 notes per minute) provided quantity and cost estimates for high-speed machines. This equipment is sometimes referred to as "vault" equipment, and is typically installed at locations such as bank branches, bank vaults, armored carrier companies, casinos, vending companies, amusement companies, retail companies, law enforcement and city offices, currency exchanges, and bill payment centers. There are two basic machine configurations: the desktop machines have one or two collection hoppers (called one pocket or two pockets) that count the currency on an automated currency sorter; currency sorters have more than two pockets and operate at much higher speeds.

OEM representatives estimated that, in addition to the equipment present at banks (and included in the estimated banking cost), there are approximately 230,573 desktop processing machines and approximately 1,383 currency sorting machines in the U.S. Although some machines may only require a software replacement ($300 for each type of machine), the OEMs believe that the most likely scenario is that all of the machines will require replacement to handle different-sized notes. The cost analysis for different-sized notes includes the machine replacement unit cost ($5,000 for desktop, $150,000 for currency sorters) as well as the software cost.

7.1.2.2. Banking/ATM

The ARINC team contacted the American Bankers Association (ABA) and worked with two leading banks (top five in terms of assets) to estimate the number of banks and branches in the U.S. There are approximately 7,400 banks in the U.S. with a combined total of approximately 78,500 bank branches. The ARINC team met with several large commercial banks to establish a generic unit-operations profile for estimating purposes that would avoid parameters unique to a specific bank. Although the ARINC team understands that there is a wide variety of organizational and operational profiles among commercial banks, this generic profile was used for this study to approximate the impact on the national banking industry.

The banking sector is considered to have a unique perspective with regard to handling and processing currency because of their focus on handling cash. They are responsible for on-site and off-site ATMs. They also deal daily with sorting and authenticating notes using mechanical equipment that must be maintained and adjusted, and is subject to breakdowns and jams in normal day-to-day use. Thus their perspective on issues involving training, human efficiency, and physical changes on machine productivity was valuable.

The commercial bank representative provided the cost impact based on a range of considerations, including bank teller efficiency, bench-top counting equipment in bank branches, ATMs, and back room operations. One of the most significant factors for banks is the inventory carrying costs of cash in their vaults, which is considered a liability. The banking representatives estimated that length of time that additional cash reserves would have to be kept in inventory is uncertain depending on the time frame for implementation of the new accommodation. The ARINC team estimated a generic bank-branch cost impact for each of the accommodations and used these generic branch estimates to determine a scaled total for all bank branches in the U.S.

Banking industry contacts stated that the recurring cost impact has two main components. First, the productivity of the bank staff decreases during the transition period from one design to another. The second and largest impact is increased inventory carrying costs because excess cash must be kept on hand during the transition period (except for machine-readable features, which would not have such an impact). The bank industry contacts estimated that the increased recurring costs could be incurred over the first three to five years after the redesign as the old designs are gradually replaced with the new designs.

The ARINC team obtained an estimated national quantity of 400,000 ATMs from the ABA in order to estimate the ATM cost. Industry OEMs provided the estimated cost for ATM modifications. They estimated that hardware modifications would be required only for the 1-D ($250 per machine) and 2-D ($450 per machine) accommodation; whereas software modifications would be required for both size changes ($75 per machine for 1-D, $100 per machine for 2-D) and tactile features ($60 per machine). They estimated there would not be a significant software change required for the machine readable features. A timeframe of approximately six months would be required to implement a software change. Between six and twelve months would be required to implement a hardware change.

7.1.2.3. End-User Industries

The ARINC team investigated the cost impact of currency accommodations on a number of end- user industries, including vending, retail, transportation, and gaming sectors (details provided in sections below). Representatives from OEMs, trade associations, and industry organizations provided estimates of the cost impact of the various currency accommodations. The equipment costs in this section are primarily for machines with direct user interface, and do not include the high-speed machines described in Section 7.1.2.1.

The ARINC team combined the estimates from multiple sources, where possible, for a ROM cost estimate. Some of the industry organizations had difficulty estimating the economic impact of certain accommodations (e.g., raised tactile features or mechanical tactile features) because they were uncertain about the new technology. In other cases (e.g., 1-D and 2-D size changes), the manufacturers and organizations were able to provide estimates based on experience with international currency designs.

Software and hardware changes for end-user machines were estimated to be similar across the market sectors. For example, the note validation equipment uses the optical scanning technology. The differences between the major vendors (in terms of market share) are not significant in terms of the cost impact of changes for the different accommodations. There are a limited number of ways that the technology might differ between OEMs, e.g., the particular recognition algorithm, the optical scanning path location, and the scan area dimensions might be slightly different. Therefore, for purposes of this study, where equipment is similar across market sectors, the costs are estimated to be the same. Detailed costs are provided in each sub-section of Section 8.

In general, industry representatives estimated that the major impact was the initial equipment investment. Once the new units were fielded, they did not anticipate significant additional costs. Therefore, the ARINC team focused the economic analysis of end-user industries on nonrecurring costs associated with the currency accommodations.

7.1.2.3.1 Vending

The ARINC team investigated the impact of the selected accommodations on the vending industry. In congressional testimony, the president and chief executive officer of the National Automatic Merchandising Association (NAMA) estimated that there were seven million vending machines in the U.S.[34] The total number of vending machines includes food, drink, cigarettes, and amusement machines. Amusement devices include video games, jukeboxes, prize crane machines, touch-screen games, pool tables, and note changers.

NAMA was a key source of quantitative information for the vending industry. Representatives from NAMA provided 2008 industry survey data[35] from member companies (vending machine operators) with the following estimates:

- Approximately 75-80% of vending machines have note acceptors.
- Approximately 92% of all currency deposited in vending machines is $1 notes (highest figure from a data submitter was 99%; lowest was 76%).
- Approximately 56% of vending machines accept denominations greater than $1 (highest figure was 90%; lowest was 0.5%).
- Approximately 44% of vending machines accept only $1 notes or just coins.

Industry OEMs provided the estimated cost for vending equipment modifications. They estimated that hardware modifications would be required only for the 1-D ($250 per machine) and 2-D ($450 per machine) accommodation; whereas software modifications would be required for size changes ($75 per machine for 1-D, $100 per machine for 2-D) and tactile features ($60 per machine). They estimated there would not be a significant software change required for the machine readable features. The quantity of equipment used for the economic analysis is the number of machines that accept denominations greater than $1 (7 million x 56% = 3.92 million). A time frame of approximately six months would be required to implement a software change. Between six and twelve months would be required to implement a hardware change.

7.1.2.3.2. Retail

The ARINC team investigated the number of retail establishments to understand the scope of this market sector. The ARINC team identified two main categories of impact from new currency designs: self-service "kiosk" machines and cash drawers to accommodate larger sized notes.

Based on discussions with OEMs for self-serve kiosk machines, along with input from large retail organizations, the ARINC team estimated that there are approximately 125,000 such machines in the U.S. There would only be a modification cost to this type of equipment if the note sizes were changed, or if a tactile or machine-readable feature was placed in the optical scan path (see Section 7.3). Based on estimates from industry OEMs, hardware modifications would be required only for the 1-D ($250 per machine) and 2-D ($450 per machine) accommodation; whereas software modifications would be required for size changes ($75 per machine for 1-D, $100 per machine for 2-D) and tactile features ($60 per machine). They estimated there would not be a significant software change required for the machine readable features. A time frame of approximately six months would be required to implement a software change. Between six and twelve months would be required to implement a hardware change.

The average size of current cash drawers in most retail establishments could accommodate both the 1-D and 2-D note sizes specified in Sections 8.1 and 8.2. However, based on discussions with major banking organizations (in terms of assets), the current drawers allow for extra room around the notes in each compartment. Because there would be very little extra room with the larger note sizes, individual retail establishments could choose to replace cash drawers (for approximately $200 each) to maintain the same amount of extra room in individual currency compartments. Alternatively, they could choose to maintain their current equipment with the tighter tolerances, and might realize an efficiency loss in cash transactions due to more awkward cash handling. Because of the high amount of uncertainty regarding cash drawer replacement, this cost is not included in the economic analyses for the 1-D and 2-D sizes.

7.1.2.3.3. Transportation

Based on discussions with a range of OEMs and with American Public Transportation Association (APTA) personnel, the ARINC team estimated that there is a minimum of 60,000 cash validation machines onboard buses and at rail, ferry, and bus stations. Based on estimates from industry OEMs, hardware modifications would be required only for the 1-D ($250 per machine) and 2-D ($450 per machine) accommodation; whereas software modifications would be required for size changes ($75 per machine for 1-D, $100 per machine for 2-D) and tactile features ($60 per machine). They estimated there would not be a significant software change required for the machine readable features. A time frame of approximately six months would be required to implement the software change and between six and twelve months for a hardware change.

The APTA data includes quantities for the 25 largest cities in the U.S. Data were not available for smaller cities, but would be expected to increase the cost analysis results proportionately for all accommodations.

As a consideration for future analyses, there are several currency processing initiatives underway to reduce the amount of cash used by the transit industry. According to APTA representatives, in most of the major markets, the local transportation authorities are trying to minimize the use of currency on public bus systems. Incentives include the use of common media among different transportation venues (e.g., bus and train), free transfers, not giving change for cash used on the bus, and charging a 'convenience' fee for using cash on the bus. In some venues (e.g., onboard New York City buses and onboard Washington DC subway trains), cash is not accepted. In these cases, cash is only accepted in the station for purchase at fare card machines. This approach greatly reduces the number of currency accepting machines required.

7.1.2.3.4. Gaming

OEM representatives estimated that the quantity of gaming cash-accepting equipment is approximately 850,000 machines. However, the gaming industry has a program underway to upgrade their equipment. Because the new equipment is manufactured by companies that serve the international marketplace, the new machines will accept larger-sized notes. Therefore, gaming industry representatives estimated that at present only about half, or 425,000, of the machines would be affected by note size changes. If a new tactile feature does not affect note size and can be designed to avoid the scan path, then no hardware change is anticipated.

The cost to replace gaming equipment hardware is slightly higher than other market sectors, approximately $850 each (includes faceplate and internal hardware). If the currency features affect the physical size of the currency, the entire currency handling unit would most likely need to be replaced. The note stacking mechanism could be affected as well as the mechanism upon which the note travels during scanning and processing. This study assumes that each of the affected machines (425,000) would require a hardware replacement. These hardware changes could take anywhere from six to twelve months to design, manufacture, test, and field.

The OEMs estimated a software modification would be required for all of the estimated 850,000 machines. They estimated the cost would be between $60 and $100 per machine depending on the nature of the accommodation. The 1-D size change would require a software modification costing approximately $75 per machine, while the cost for a software modification for the 2-D size change would be approximately $100 per machine. The software modification required for a mechanical, raised, or embedded feature, as considered in this study, would be closer to approximately $60 per machine. The OEMs estimated that approximately three to six months would be required to implement the software change, depending on the complexity of the change.

7.1.3. U.S. Individuals

The ARINC team considered the impact that each of the accommodations would have on the general U.S. population. For some of the accommodations, such as addition of printed features or machine-readable features, the general public would not incur any direct cost as a result of changes to the currency. Some of the accommodations, such as larger sizes, might have a direct impact if individuals choose to purchase new wallets or money clips.

7.1.4. Cost Analysis Summary

Section 8 includes a cost analysis summary table for each of the selected accommodations, presented in constant fiscal year 2009 dollars, in millions. The cost summary tables identify the estimated initial nonrecurring costs by market sector. The BEP, FRB, and the banking industry representatives also estimated the annual recurring cost impact of each accommodation. However, it was unclear how long these higher recurring costs would continue, due to uncertainty in the time period over which the accommodations would be implemented. The other market sectors stated that, in general, once they had made the initial investment, they did not expect significant recurring cost impacts from these accommodations.

7.2. Benefit Analysis Methodology

The ARINC team performed an assessment of the benefits of the selected accommodations. The analysts based these assessments on the results of the focus group comments (Section 3), survey results (Section 4), and usability testing results (Section 6).

The ARINC team based the benefit evaluations on how well the accommodation addressed the transaction scenarios and issues that focus group and survey participants identified. Participants identified three currency usage scenarios as the most important—(1) transactions with no other people in close proximity, (2) transactions while in line (with people waiting), and (3) quick inventory of wallet or purse. Existing challenges for blind and VI people in the use of U.S. currency include (1) receiving the wrong denomination in change or providing the wrong denomination in a transaction, (2) social stigma caused by the time required for them to correctly identify a currency denomination, and (3) the potential for problems inherent in interactions with strangers.

The ARINC team measured usability in terms of two parameters: (1) speed to denominate currency and (2) the accuracy of the recognition for both blind and VI participants. Tactile features, note size changes, and reader devices were the primary focus of usability testing because these are the categories of accommodations with the most promise for enhancing currency denomination by the blind and VI.

The speed and accuracy results for each accommodation are conservative measures of benefit because the usability test participants were new to the accommodation, currency, or device and had limited familiarization time. Speed and accuracy would be expected to increase with extensive use, up to certain limits that have not been precisely determined. The speed and accuracy of currency reader devices, even with ideal usage, is limited more significantly by device technology than by user familiarity.

7.3. Other Considerations

In addition to the economic and benefit analyses, the ARINC team considered each accommodation with respect to the impact on other non-cost parameters, where relevant.

Representatives of cash machine OEMs indicated that the placement of tactile or machine- readable features could have a significant impact on the ability of the validating hardware to correctly identify denomination. Most note validation equipment in the market today uses optical technology. The optical scan path is at the center of the note, extending from top to bottom, and across the length to about one inch from each edge. If the tactile or machine-readable features are located outside of the optical scan path, little or no change to the hardware would be required. However, if the features change the appearance of the image in the optical path, there could be a significant impact on the equipment's ability to accurately validate a note.

OEM representatives also estimated that the average time to field software changes (including software modification and debugging time) would range from three months for minor changes to six months for more complicated changes. The more complex changes would be correspondingly more expensive. OEM participants reported that only software changes would be required for cases where the accommodations were similar to those implemented for their European-design hardware. They estimated that hardware changes for other equipment could take up to a year, provided there was no manufacturing backlog. The ARINC team was not able to obtain information on what quantities of new equipment would produce a manufacturing backlog situation, but it remains a potential risk to timely implementation for any new feature requiring a hardware change.

Individuals who already own reader devices could be affected by the addition of any accommodation and may have to replace or upgrade currency readers to work with a new currency feature.

Gaming industry representatives and OEMs described new technologies being introduced into the gaming industry that would eventually replace most currency handling machines. This new technology is referred to as ticket-in, ticket-out (TITO). These new machines accept and dispense a bar-coded ticket that takes the place of currency. The introduction of these devices, in the long term, would significantly reduce the number of cash handling machines. Industry representatives estimated that eventually all of the currency-based machines will be replaced with TITO machines, but the time frame for complete transition is uncertain. The longer-term introduction of this technology places it beyond the scope of this study, but could be an impact for future analyses.

8. ECONOMIC ANALYSIS OF SELECTED ACCOMMODATIONS

8.1. Economic Analysis of 1-D Sizes

For the purposes of the economic analysis, the ARINC team (together with the BEP), defined prototype 1-D sizes as a set of notes where the $1 Federal Reserve note is the basis for width and the minimum length, and the maximum length would be 180 mm (typical maximum length for the printing and processing equipment planned for purchase by the BEP).

The minimum length was based on requirements of the Omnibus Appropriations Act of 2009: "*None of the funds appropriated in this Act or otherwise available to the Department of the Treasury or the Bureau of Engraving and Printing may be used to redesign the $1 Federal Reserve note.*" The maximum length was established after discussions with manufacturers of international equipment and the BEP about the physical limitations of their equipment.

The ARINC team used these limits for purposes of this study. The prototype 1-D sizes (described in Section 6.4.1) had lengths ranging from 156 mm (length of existing U.S. currency) to 180 mm (typical maximum length for cash-handling equipment). This allowed for approximately 4 mm between each denomination. Appendix K provides an illustration of the 1-D currency sizes.

8.1.1. Cost Analysis

Table 8-1 in Section 8.1.1.4 provides a summary of the costs for each organization or market sector discussed below. Sections 8.1.1.1 through 8.1.1.3 provide the assumptions specific to the 1-D accommodation.

8.1.1.1. U.S. Government

Based on the assumption stated at the beginning of Section 7 that larger sheet size equipment would be operational at BEP, the 1-D size change would not require the BEP to purchase any equipment unique to incorporating this accommodation. However, this accommodation would result in significant increases in paper and ink costs because fewer of the larger-sized notes could be printed on each sheet. Fewer notes per sheet would equate to more sheets printed to meet the FRB's yearly currency order requirements, and would result in a substantial increase in paper costs. Likewise, larger-sized notes would require more ink to be used on a per-note basis, which would also result in increased ink costs.

The efficiency of all production operations would be negatively impacted if the physical nature of the note design required all operations to decrease their operating speeds to properly print and process the new notes. Slower operating speeds would require more production shifts at all operations, requiring additional staff to run the additional shifts. In addition, the efficiency decrease would place a constraint on overprinting capacity, requiring the BEP to purchase additional overprinting equipment to meet the FRB's currency order requirements.

The BEP estimated that the initial nonrecurring cost to implement the 1-D size differences would be approximately $179 million, including research and development and public education. The resulting increase in BEP annual recurring costs would be approximately $37 million per year.

The FRB estimated that the cost to modify their equipment would be approximately $250 million and take two to three years to develop and deploy. However, if the equipment could not be modified, and new equipment was required (this is uncertain), the cost could be as much as $400 million and could take approximately five years to implement. Because of the uncertainty in the new equipment requirements, the $250 million modification cost is used in Table 8-1. The size differences would also affect the machine processing speed. The FRB estimated that the overall speed would need to be decreased as much as 10%, resulting in a corresponding increase in processing cost. Finally, the larger note sizes would reduce the number of notes that could be stored in currency transport devices and vaults, necessitating changes to the current physical processes. The FRB estimated that the impact on annual recurring costs could be up to $2 million for decreased productivity of processing different sized notes.

8.1.1.2. U.S. Market Sectors

8.1.1.2.1. High-Speed Machines

One of the top three OEMs (in terms of U.S. market share) for high-speed cash processing machines provided quantity and cost estimates for high-speed machines. They estimated that for a 1-D note size change, both the desktop and currency sorter machine hardware and software would most likely need to be replaced (approximately 230,573 desktop processing machines and 1,383 currency sorting machines). The cost to replace all machines would be approximately $1.4 billion (includes hardware and software cost). Should hardware replacement not be required, the approximate cost just for the software change (the OEMs stated this is unlikely, therefore this cost is not included in Table 8-1) could be as low as $70 million.

8.1.1.2.2. Banking/ATM

Commercial banking contacts estimated that the primary cost elements of a length-only change would be inventory carrying costs, training of tellers, hardware and software modifications to cash discriminator equipment, and retooling automated high-speed processing equipment. The banking representatives estimated that additional cash reserves would have to be kept in inventory, and the cost of carrying that additional inventory would be significant. The total estimated nonrecurring cost for hardware and software changes for approximately 7,400 banks was estimated to be $1.38 billion.

The annual recurring cost, which includes a 20% growth in inventory carrying costs from having excess cash on hand, as well as a higher frequency of equipment interruption due to jams, was estimated to be approximately $4.35 billion.

The estimated cost to upgrade the estimated 400,000 ATMs for a 1-D size change was approximately $250 per machine for hardware changes, and approximately $75 per machine for software updates.

8.1.1.2.3. Vending

As discussed in Section 7.1.2.3.1, industry representatives provided general information from across the end-user industries with respect to cash-handling equipment. The collection box and the path for scanning the note are the physical limitations. In the case of a length change less than 180 mm, it is possible that only the currency collection box would need to be modified.

According to congressional testimony by a NAMA executive, notes that are significantly longer than current U.S. notes would not fit into the current storage boxes for note validation devices and could cause jamming in the note transport mechanism.[36] Industry representatives also indicated that, depending on the configuration of the hardware that is already present, the note collection box in the back of the machine may have to be modified.

Based on input from a range of OEMs and vending community members, the ARINC team estimated that there are approximately 3.92 million units in the U.S. that accept notes in denominations greater than $1, the average cost of the required software changes would be approximately $75 per machine, and the average cost for bill acceptor faceplate and internal hardware changes would be approximately $250 per machine. The total estimated cost would be $1.27 billion.

8.1.1.2.4. Retail

Based on discussions with OEMs, the estimated quantity of retail sales self-serve equipment is approximately 125,000 machines. Some of the existing equipment could handle a nominal increase in the length of existing currency. However, because ultimate dimensions of a 1-D size change as tested in this study (180 mm) would exceed the nominal increase, the ARINC team assumed that a hardware replacement would be required for all machines. The 1-D size change would require an internal hardware replacement cost of approximately $250 each and software update cost of approximately $75 each.

As discussed in Section 7.1.2.3.2, the total quantity of cash drawers that retailers would replace to accommodate longer notes is uncertain. The cost per cash drawer is approximately $200. This cost is not shown in Table 8-1 due to the uncertainty of how many retailers would replace their equipment versus how many would decide to operate with slightly lower productivity.

8.1.1.2.5. Transportation

The industry representatives estimated that the 1-D size change could require new hardware, with a replacement cost of approximately $250 per machine, and a software modification of approximately $75 per machine, for each of the estimated 60,000 machines.

8.1.1.2.6. Gaming

Based on discussions with OEMs, the estimated cost to replace the hardware to accept 1-D sized notes was approximately $850 per machine (for estimated 425,000 affected machines), with a software upgrade cost of approximately $75 (all estimated 850,000 machines).

8.1.1.3. U.S. Individuals

The direct cost to the general U.S. population for 1-D size changes would be primarily the cost of cash-holding accessories such as wallets or money clips. Longer notes could be folded to fit in existing accessories. However, individuals may prefer a variety of solutions ranging from folding to purchasing new cash-holding accessories; the cost of such new accessories could be expected to vary from person to person. The ARINC team did not include the potential cost of these accessories because of the uncertainty in the number of individuals affected.

8.1.1.4. Cost Analysis Summary

Table 8-1 shows a summary of the economic analysis of 1-D size notes.

8.1.2. Benefit Analysis

The ARINC team assessed the benefits of note size differences through focus groups, survey responses, and usability testing of notes with 1-D size changes. A number of foreign currencies (including the Swiss franc, and Australian dollar) vary note length size by denomination.

The results of the usability testing for blind participants, described in detail in Section 6 of this report, indicate that currencies with 1-D size difference were associated with slower and less accurate denomination than currencies with 2-D size differences

Varying note size by denomination directly addresses the key usage scenarios for quick inventory and public transactions, for blind and VI people. Regardless of the scenario, the longer a currency denomination accommodation takes to use, the less desirable that accommodation becomes. Seventy-two percent of survey respondents cited "feeling rushed" during cash transactions using current U.S. currency in public, and many focus group participants mentioned the same feeling, especially when there were people waiting in line behind them.

As described in Section 4.2.4 of this report, over half of the survey respondents said that notes of different sizes would make U.S. currency easier for them to use. A 1995 NRC report[37] compared the denomination accuracy of 1-D size differences for blind users. According to that report, a 12 mm change in length for each denomination results in an accuracy rate of 75% compared to a significantly higher 90% accuracy rate when note sizes were varied in both length and width.

The usability test results in Section 6.5 of this report generally confirmed these findings, with a clear trend that the larger the size difference between denominations, the faster the participants could correctly identify a denomination. For example, blind usability test participants denominated Swiss francs (11 mm length differences) with an speed of 7.4 seconds at 65% average accuracy, compared with an average speed of 12.9 seconds and average accuracy of 48% for Australian dollars (7 mm length differences). The 1-D sizes with approximate 4 mm length differences resulted in similar speed (9 seconds), but with average accuracy of only 41% (many participants indicated they were merely guessing).

8.1.3. Other Considerations

Usability testing participants who own reader devices indicated that even for the accommodations that worked well, they still might choose to keep their current devices to use at home. Individuals such as these, who now use currency readers, could be adversely affected by 1-D size differences, based on comments from usability testing participants. Current owners of reader devices could be required to replace or upgrade them to work with a 1-D size change.

Although the study did not investigate the impact of size changes on the general U.S. population, a 1-D size change would be a significant departure from current U.S. currency. BEP public education costs are expected to be higher for size changes than for the other accommodations, as a wide range of consumers would be affected by such a change.

The ARINC team researched information on the methodology for establishing size differences along one dimension versus two dimensions. The Reserve Bank of Australia discussed the rationale for their currency design and indicated that they had determined that a change in one dimension would be sufficient to allow blind people to denominate currency. The change also facilitated development of an inexpensive measuring device (similar to a small plastic ruler).

Table 8-1. Economic Analysis of 1-D Notes (FY 2009 $M)

Organization/ Market Sector	Nonrecurring Cost	Recurring Annual Cost
BEP	$179.0	$37.0
FRB	$250.0	$2.0
High Speed - Desktop	$1,222.0	$0.0
High Speed - Currency Sorting	$207.9	$0.0
Banking	$1,383.4	$4,349.7
ATM	$130.0	$0.0
Vending	$1,274.0	$0.0
Retail	$40.6	$0.0
Transportation	$19.5	$0.0
Gaming	$425.0	$0.0
TOTAL	**$5,131.4**	**$4,388.7**

8.1.4. Conclusions – 1-D Sizes

The ARINC team performed a cost analysis and a qualitative benefit analysis of 1-D sizes (i.e., variation of only the length by denomination) as an accommodation for currency denomination by blind people:

- The ARINC team estimated combined Government and industry costs of more than $9.5 billion for nonrecurring investment and annual recurring costs for the first year.
- Usability tests of currency with 1-D sizes (i.e., Australian, Swiss, and the prototype 1-D sizes) indicated that blind participants were able to achieve only moderate denomination accuracy (averages ranged between 41% for the prototype 1-D and 65% for the Swiss as shown in Figures 6-53 and 6-54), even though the denomination speed was relatively good (averages ranged between 7.4 for the Swiss and 12.9 seconds for the Australian sizes, see Figures 5-51 and 6-52). The accuracy results were best with the currency having the largest difference between sizes (Swiss), and the worst with the prototype 1-D sizes, which had the smallest difference between sizes.

8.2. Economic Analysis of 2-D Sizes

For the purposes of the economic analysis, the ARINC team (together with the BEP), defined 2-D sizes as a set of notes where the $1 Federal Reserve note is the basis for the minimum length and width, the maximum length would be 180 mm, and the maximum width would be 82 mm (typical maximum length and width for the printing and processing equipment planned for purchase by the BEP).

The minimum length and width were based on requirements of the Omnibus Appropriations Act of 2009:"*None of the funds appropriated in this Act or otherwise available to the Department of the Treasury or the Bureau of Engraving and Printing may be used to redesign the $1 Federal Reserve note.*" The maximum length and width were established after discussions with manufacturers of international equipment and the BEP about the physical limitations of their equipment.

The ARINC team used these limits for purposes of this study. The prototype 2-D sizes (described in Section 6.4.2) had lengths ranging from 156 mm to 180 mm; and widths ranging from 66 mm (the width of existing U.S. currency) to 82 mm. This allowed larger size differences between each denomination (the basic sizes are short-narrow, short-wide, medium-narrow, medium-wide, long-narrow and long-wide). Appendix K illustrates the 2-D currency sizes.

8.2.1. Cost Analysis

Table 8-2 in Section 8.2.1.4 provides a summary of the costs for each organization or market sector discussed below. Sections 8.2.1.1 through 8.2.1.3 provide the assumptions specific to the 2-D accommodation.

8.2.1.1. U.S. Government

Based on the assumption, stated at the beginning of Section 7, that larger sheet size equipment would be operational at BEP, the 2-D sizes would not require the BEP to purchase any equipment unique to incorporating this feature. However, this accommodation would result in significant increases in paper and ink costs because fewer of the larger-sized notes could be printed on each sheet. Fewer notes per sheet would equate to more sheets printed to meet the FRB's yearly currency order requirements, and would result in a substantial increase in paper costs. Likewise, larger-sized notes would require more ink to be used on a per-note basis, which would also result in increased ink costs.

The efficiency of all production operations would be negatively impacted if the physical nature of the 2-D sizes required all operations to decrease their operating speeds to properly print and process the new notes. Slower operating speeds would require more production shifts at all operations, requiring additional staff to run the additional shifts. In addition, the efficiency decrease would place a constraint on intaglio and overprinting capacity, requiring the BEP to purchase additional equipment to meet the FRB's currency order requirements.

The BEP estimated that the initial nonrecurring cost to implement the 2-D size differences would be approximately $202 million. The resulting increase in BEP annual recurring costs would be approximately $70 million per year.

The FRB estimated that the cost to modify their equipment would be approximately $250 million and take two to three years to develop and deploy. However, if the equipment could not be modified, and new equipment was required (this is uncertain), the cost could be as much as $400 million and could take approximately five years to implement. Because of the uncertainty in the new equipment requirements, the $250 million modification cost is used in Table 8-2. The size differences would also affect the machine processing speed. The FRB estimated that the overall speed would need to be decreased as much as 10%, resulting in a corresponding increase in processing cost. Finally, the larger note sizes would reduce the number of notes that could be stored in currency transport devices and vaults, necessitating changes to the current physical processes. The FRB estimated that the impact on annual recurring costs could be up to $2 million for decreased productivity of processing different sized notes.

8.2.1.2. U.S. Market Sectors

8.2.1.2.1. High-Speed Machines

One of the top three OEMs (in terms of U.S. market share) for high-speed cash processing machines provided quantity and cost estimates for high-speed machines. They estimated that for a 2-D note size change, both the desktop and currency sorting machine hardware and software would need to be replaced (approximately 230,573 desktop processing machines and approximately 1,383 currency sorting machines). The cost to replace all machines would be approximately $1.4 billion (includes hardware and software cost). Should hardware replacement not be required, the approximate cost for a software change only (the OEMs stated this is unlikely, therefore this cost is not included in Table 8-2) could be as low as $70 million.

8.2.1.2.2. Banking/ATM

Commercial banking contacts estimated that the primary cost elements of a length and width change would be inventory carrying costs, training of tellers, hardware and software modifications to cash discriminator equipment, and retooling of automated high-speed processing equipment. The banking representatives estimated that additional cash reserves would have to be kept in inventory, and the cost of carrying that additional inventory would be significant. The total estimated nonrecurring cost for hardware and software changes for approximately 7,400 banks was estimated to be approximately the same as for the 1-D sizes, $1.38 billion.

The annual recurring cost, which includes a 20% growth in inventory carrying costs from having excess cash on hand, as well as a higher frequency of equipment interruption due to jams, was estimated to be approximately $4.3 billion.

The estimated cost to upgrade the estimated 400,000 ATMs for a 2-D size change is approximately $450 per machine for hardware changes and approximately $100 per machine for software updates.

8.2.1.2.3. Vending

Industry representatives estimated that both software and hardware modifications would be required for most equipment to accommodate notes with variable length and width. Based on input from a range of OEMs and vending community members, the ARINC team estimated that there are approximately 3.92 million units in the U.S. that accept notes in denominations greater than $1. The hardware costs for a 2-D change would be greater than the cost for a 1-D change, due to changes required in the faceplate, note acceptor mechanism, and other equipment processes. The average cost of the software changes would be approximately $100 per machine and the average cost for faceplate and internal hardware changes would be approximately $450 per machine.

8.2.1.2.4. Retail

Based on discussions with OEMs, the estimated quantity of retail sales self-serve equipment is approximately 125,000 machines. Some of the existing equipment could handle a nominal increase in the length of existing currency. However, because the ultimate dimensions of a 2-D size change as tested in this study (82 mm by 180 mm) would exceed the nominal increase, the ARINC team assumed that a hardware replacement would be required for all machines. The 2-D size change would require internal hardware replacement cost of approximately $450 each and software update cost of approximately $100 each.

As discussed in Section 7.1.2.3.2, the total quantity of cash drawers that retailers would replace to accommodate larger notes is uncertain. The cost per cash drawer is approximately $200. This cost is not shown in Table 8-2 due to the uncertainty of how many retailers would replace their equipment versus how many would decide to operate with slightly lower productivity.

8.2.1.2.5. Transportation
The industry representatives estimated that a 2-D size change would require new hardware, with a replacement cost of approximately $450 per machine and a software modification of approximately $100 per machine, for each of the estimated 60,000 machines.

8.2.1.2.6. Gaming
Based on discussions with OEMs, the estimated cost to replace the hardware to accept 2-D sized notes was approximately $850 per machine (for estimated 425,000 affected machines), with a software upgrade cost of approximately $100 per machine (all estimated 850,000 machines).

8.2.1.3. U.S. Individuals
The direct cost to the general U.S. population for 2-D size changes would be primarily the cost of cash-holding accessories such as wallets or money clips. Longer and wider notes could require folding to fit in existing accessories. However, individuals could prefer a wide variety of solutions ranging from folding to purchasing new cash-holding accessories; the cost of such new accessories could be expected to vary from person to person. The ARINC team did not include the potential cost of these accessories because of the uncertainty in the number of individuals affected.

8.2.1.4. Cost Analysis Summary
Table 8-2 shows a summary of the economic analysis of 2-D size notes.

Table 8-2. Economic Analysis of 2-D Notes (FY 2009 $M)

Organization/ Market Sector	Nonrecurring Cost	Recurring Annual Cost
BEP	$202.0	$69.9
FRB	$250.0	$2.0
High Speed - Desktop	$1,222.0	$0.0
High Speed - Currency Sorting	$207.9	$0.0
Banking	$1,383.4	$4,349.7
ATM	$220.0	$0.0
Vending	$2,156.0	$0.0
Retail	$68.8	$0.0
Transportation	$33.0	$0.0
Gaming	$446.3	$0.0
TOTAL	**$6,189.4**	**$4,421.6**

8.2.2. Benefit Analysis

The ARINC team assessed the benefits of note size variation through focus groups, surveys, and usability testing of notes with 2-D size changes. As described in Section 4 of this report, over one half of the survey respondents said that notes of different sizes would make U.S. currency easier for them to use. The 1995 NRC report[38] compared the denomination accuracy of size differences for blind users. According to that report, up to 75% accuracy could be achieved with 1-D size variations compared to a significantly higher 90% accuracy rate with 2-D note sizes. The ARINC usability testing results as shown in Section 6.5 indicated that blind participants were able to denominate Swedish kronor, which incorporate significant size variation in length and width, more rapidly than any other currency (or prototype accommodation) tested. Blind participants took longer to denominate currencies with smaller size differences (e.g., UK pound and euro) than for the kronor.

Varying note size by denomination directly addresses the key usage scenarios for quick inventory and public transactions, for blind and VI people. Regardless of the scenario, the longer a currency denomination accommodation takes to use, the less desirable that accommodation will be. Seventy-two percent of survey respondents cited "feeling rushed" during cash transactions in public, and many focus group participants mentioned the same feeling, especially when there were people waiting in line behind them.

8.2.3. Other Considerations

Usability testing participants who own reader devices indicated that even for the accommodations that worked well, they still could choose to keep their current devices to use at home. Individuals such as these, who now use currency readers, could be adversely affected by 2-D size differences, based on comments from usability testing participants. Current owners of reader devices could be required to replace or upgrade them to work with a 2-D change.

Although the study did not investigate the impact of size changes on the general U.S. population, a 2-D size change would be a radical departure from current U.S. currency. BEP public education costs are expected to be higher than for the other accommodations, as a wide range of consumers would be affected by such a change.

8.2.4. Conclusions – 2-D Sizes

The ARINC team performed a cost analysis and a qualitative benefit analysis of 2-D sizes (i.e., variation of both length and width) as an accommodation for currency denomination by blind people:

- The ARINC team estimated combined Government and industry costs of more than $10.6 billion for nonrecurring investment and first-year recurring costs.
- Distinct 2-D note size differences (Swedish kronor) resulted in the highest average speed performance (7.2 seconds) and accuracy (73%) for blind usability test participants for all of the currency types with size differences (see Section 6.5). Smaller size differences (UK pound, euro, and prototype 2-D sizes), resulted in slower speeds (averages ranged between 10.1 and 10.8 seconds) and lower accuracy (averages ranged from 60% to 63%).

8.3. Economic Analysis of Mechanical Tactile Features

For the purposes of this study, the ARINC team (with approval from the BEP) investigated mechanical tactile features in the form of notches along the edges of the notes (as used in the usability testing).

8.3.1. Cost Analysis

Table 8-3 in Section 8.3.1.4 provides a summary of the costs for each organization or market sector discussed below. Sections 8.3.1.1 through 8.3.1.3 provide the assumptions specific to the mechanical tactile feature accommodation.

8.3.1.1. U.S. Government

As noted in Section 5.1.4.2, representatives from Crane & Co., Inc. indicated that adding mechanical features as part of the paper manufacturing process has a potential for paper debris interfering with the quality control process. The higher rejection rate would cause the cost of paper manufacturing to increase and that cost would be passed on directly to the BEP.

BEP estimated that they could purchase equipment that could be made capable of cutting notches or holes to create a mechanical tactile feature at the end of their manufacturing process. Additional staff would be required to operate this equipment. Since this feature is totally machine-generated, no additional material unique to this feature would be needed.

The incorporation of notches would result in the generation of additional spoilage during the production process, increasing the overall cost of existing raw materials (paper and ink). The complexity of producing notes increases as more features are added to the production process, increasing the likelihood of spoilage. The spoilage increase would require additional production shifts at all operations. (As overall yield decreases, more sheets would need to be printed to meet the FRB's currency order requirements.) Labor and variable overhead costs could increase as a result of these additional shifts.

The efficiency of overprinting operations would be negatively impacted because the physical nature of the feature would require decreased operating speeds to properly print and process notes that incorporate this new feature. Slower operating speeds would require more production shifts, requiring additional staff to run the additional shifts. In addition, the efficiency decrease would place an equipment constraint on overprinting capacity, requiring the BEP to purchase additional overprinting equipment to meet the FRB's currency order requirements.

The initial nonrecurring cost for BEP to implement a mechanical tactile feature such as notches would be approximately $95 million. The resulting increase in BEP annual recurring costs would be approximately $8.5 million per year.

The FRB estimated that this type of feature would require sensor software and hardware modifications to verify the correct feature is present and usable. The anticipated sensor software and minor hardware modifications could cost up to $3 million according to the FRB. The software change would take one year to implement and a hardware change would take two years to implement. If a current sensor could not be modified, a new sensor would need to be acquired, which could cost up to $32 million and take four years to develop and deploy. This is the cost reflected in Table 8-3 as the most likely scenario. However, modifications to processing equipment could be required, which would cost up to $4 million and take two years to develop and deploy, but this is more uncertain according to the FRB, therefore these costs are not included in Table 8-3. The FRB did not provide estimates of the annual recurring cost due to uncertainty with respect to specifics on an actual mechanical feature design.

8.3.1.2. U.S. Market Sectors

8.3.1.2.1. High-Speed Machines

One of the top three OEMs (in terms of market share) for high-speed cash processing machines provided quantity and cost estimates for high-speed machines (approximately 230,573 desktop processing machines and 1,383 currency sorting machines). They estimated that for a mechanical tactile feature, only a software change would be required for the desktop and currency sorting machines, at approximately $300 per machine.

8.3.1.2.2. Banking/ATMs

Commercial banking representatives expressed concern about a potential decrease in note durability as a result of this feature. In their experience, notes currently circulating with accidental physical defects jam mechanical equipment such as counting and authentication equipment and ATMs. These defects also tend to propagate into tears that further diminish processing speed and efficiency. Either of these impacts would represent additional fixed costs to purchase more machines to maintain current processing rates and additional recurring costs to clear jams and perform maintenance.

Commercial banking representatives estimated that the primary cost elements of adding notches or perforations would be inventory carrying costs, training of tellers, hardware and software modifications to cash discriminator equipment, and retooling of automated high-speed processing equipment (similar to impact of 1-D and 2-D size changes). The total estimated nonrecurring cost for hardware and software changes for approximately 7,400 banks was estimated to be $1.37 billion. The annual recurring cost, which includes a 20% growth in inventory carrying costs from having excess cash on hand, as well as equipment interruption due to jams (higher than the 1-D and 2-D size changes), could be as high as approximately $4.7 billion.

The estimated cost to upgrade the estimated 400,000 ATMs for a mechanical feature was estimated to be approximately $60 per machine for software updates. No hardware changes were estimated to be required.

8.3.1.2.3. Vending

Industry representatives provided general information from across the end-user industries with respect to cash-handling equipment. The industry representatives reported that only software modifications would be required for most equipment to accommodate notes with mechanical features. Based on input from a range of OEMs and vending community members, the ARINC team estimated that there are approximately 3.92 million units in the U.S. that accept notes in denominations greater than $1 and the average unit cost of the required software changes would be approximately $60.

8.3.1.2.4. Retail

Industry representatives provided general information from across the end-user industries with respect to cash-handling equipment. The industry representatives reported that only software modifications would be required for most equipment to accommodate notes with mechanical features. Based on input from a range of OEMs and retail community members, the ARINC team estimated that there are 125,000 retail self-serve machines, and the average unit cost of the required software changes is approximately $60.

There would not be any requirement to change the cash drawers for this accommodation.

8.3.1.2.5. Transportation

The industry representatives estimated that only software modifications would be required for most equipment to accommodate notes with mechanical features. Based on input from a range of OEMs and transit community association personnel, the ARINC team estimated that the average unit cost of the required software changes was approximately $60 for each of the estimated 60,000 machines.

8.3.1.2.6. Gaming

Based on discussions with OEMs, the estimated cost to upgrade the software to accept mechanical features was approximately $60 per machine (all estimated 850,000 machines). No hardware changes were anticipated.

8.3.1.3. U.S. Individuals

The ARINC team did not identify any direct costs to the general U.S. population resulting from the introduction of mechanical tactile features.

8.3.1.4. Cost Analysis Summary

Table 8-3 shows a summary of the economic analysis of mechanical tactile features.

Table 8-3. Economic Analysis of Mechanical Tactile Feature Notes (FY 2009 $M)

Organization/Market Sector	Nonrecurring Cost	Recurring Annual Cost
BEP	$94.5	$8.5
FRB	$32.0	N/A
High Speed - Desktop	$69.2	$0.0
High Speed - Currency Sorting	$0.4	$0.0
Banking	$1,377.0	$4,722.9
ATM	$24.0	$0.0
Vending	$235.2	$0.0
Retail	$7.5	$0.0
Transportation	$3.6	$0.0
Gaming	$51.0	$0.0
TOTAL	**$1,894.4**	**$4,731.4**

8.3.2. Benefit Analysis

Mechanical tactile features, including notched corners and perforations could address the key usage scenarios (i.e., quick inventory and public transactions) for both blind and VI people. As described in Section 4 of this report, over one half of the survey respondents said that they believed a tactile accommodation would be beneficial. Under most usage scenarios, the user could still have to at least partially remove the notes from their wallet or billfold to denominate notes using the notches tested. However, many participants commented that they preferred the notches to the other accommodations tested, and that they anticipated they would also use them in line at a store to confirm the change received from a cashier.

Results of usability tests on notched prototype samples indicated that blind participants derived significant benefit from notched tactile accommodations. The participants were more accurate in denominating the notches than any other currency or prototype feature in this study. The participants were slightly faster using the Swedish kronor and the Swiss Franc (average of 7.2 and 7.4 seconds, respectively), but they had average accuracy of only 73% and 65%, respectively.

8.3.3. Other Considerations

Individuals who use currency readers could also be adversely affected by notches or perforations, depending on whether or not the features affect the area of the note used by the device to identify denominations. People with tactile sensitivity impairments may not be able to perceive a tactile feature, and thus would still require a device. Current owners of reader devices could be required to replace or upgrade them to work with physical tactile features.

Although the ARINC team did not investigate the impact of notches or perforations on the general U.S. population, the notches tested would not present a major departure from current U.S. currency because they could be incorporated into existing note designs.

According to major cash machine OEMs (in terms of market share), as long as the perforations were not larger than 1/8 inch in diameter, and not within the scan path of the hardware, only a software change would be required. For larger perforations or features in the scan path, hardware changes could be required as well. For paper handling efficiency reasons, the OEMs did not endorse mechanical features such as notches along the edges of the note. They felt this type of feature had the potential to create paper handling issues such as jams, feeding errors, and note transport problems.

8.3.4. Conclusions – Mechanical Tactile Features

The ARINC team performed a cost analysis and a qualitative benefit analysis of mechanical tactile features (i.e., notches) as an accommodation for currency denomination by blind people.

- The ARINC team estimated combined Government and industry costs of more than $6.6 billion for nonrecurring investment and first-year recurring costs.
- Blind usability test participants were more accurate in denominating notches than any other feature or currency tested (average of 89%). Most blind participants were able to denominate the system of notches quickly (average of 8.5 seconds), slightly slower than the Swedish kronor and the Swiss franc (which had lower accuracy than the notches).

8.4. Economic Analysis of Raised Tactile Features

For the purposes of this study, the ARINC team (with approval from the BEP) investigated raised tactile features as similar to the dots present in the Canadian notes or intaglio ink printed bars, with similar height above the paper substrate.

8.4.1. Cost Analysis

Table 8-4 in Section 8.4.1.4 provides a summary of the costs for each organization or market sector discussed below. Sections 8.4.1.1 through 8.4.1.3 provide the assumptions specific to the raised tactile feature accommodation.

8.4.1.1. U.S. Government

A raised tactile feature would require the BEP to purchase new equipment to produce this feature. Additional staff would be required to operate this new equipment. New raw materials unique to the generation of this feature would also be required. The incorporation of this new operation would result in the generation of additional spoilage during the production process, increasing the BEP's overall cost of existing raw materials (paper and ink). The complexity of producing notes increases as more features are added to the production process, increasing the likelihood of spoilage. The spoilage increase would require additional production shifts at all operations. (As overall yield declines, more sheets would need to be printed to meet the FRB's currency order requirements.)

The raised tactile feature could also negatively impact the efficiency of the manufacturing operations subsequent to the tactile-generating operation. The physical nature of this new feature would require these operations to slow down production rates to properly process these notes, requiring additional production shifts for these operations. As additional production shifts are required, additional staff would be required to run these shifts. In addition, the efficiency decrease would place an equipment constraint on overprinting capacity, requiring the BEP to purchase additional overprinting equipment to meet the FRB's currency order requirements.

The initial nonrecurring cost for BEP to implement a raised tactile feature such as dots or bars would be approximately $95 million. The resulting increase in BEP annual recurring costs would be approximately $12 million per year.

The FRB estimated that this type of feature would require sensor software and hardware modifications to verify the correct feature is present and usable. These sensor software and minor hardware modifications could cost up to $3 million and take up to one year to implement. If a current sensor could not be modified, a new sensor would need to be acquired, which could cost up to $28 million and take four years to develop and deploy. This is the cost reflected in Table 8-4 as the most likely scenario. A hardware change could take two years to implement.

8.4.1.2. U.S. Market Sectors

8.4.1.2.1. High-Speed Machines

One of the top three OEMs (in terms of market share) for high-speed cash processing machines provided quantity and cost estimates for high-speed machines (approximately

230,573 desktop processing machines and 1,383 currency sorting machines). They estimated that for a raised tactile feature, only a software change would be required for the desktop and currency sorting machines, at approximately $300 per machine.

8.4.1.2.2. Banking/ATMs

Commercial banking representatives estimated that the primary cost driver of raised features would be similar to that of the mechanical features such as notches, increasing the amount of manual processing in their vaults (high-speed machines). These features would also require training of tellers, hardware and software modifications to cash discriminator equipment, and retooling of automated high-speed processing equipment (i.e., same as for length only and length and width size changes). The total estimated nonrecurring cost for hardware and software changes for approximately 7,400 banks was estimated to be $1.37 billion.

The annual recurring cost, which includes a 20% growth in inventory carrying costs from having excess cash on hand, as well as equipment interruption due to jams (higher than the 1-D and 2-D size changes), was estimated to be approximately $4.7 billion.

The estimated cost to upgrade the estimated 400,000 ATMs for a raised tactile feature was approximately $60 per machine for software updates. No hardware changes were estimated to be required.

8.4.1.2.3. Vending

Industry representatives provided general information from across the end-user industries with respect to cash-handling equipment. The industry representatives reported that only software modifications would be required for most equipment to accommodate notes with raised tactile features. Based on input from a range of OEMs and vending community members, the ARINC team estimated that there are approximately 3.92 million units in the U.S. that accept notes in denominations greater than $1, and the average unit cost of the required software changes would be approximately $60.

8.4.1.2.4. Retail

Industry representatives provided general information from across the end-user industries with respect to cash-handling equipment. Discussions with the Bank of Canada indicate that the raised feature on their currency did not cause notable equipment problems. Industry representatives reported that only software modifications would be required for most equipment to accommodate notes with raised features. Based on input from a range of OEMs and retail community members, the ARINC team estimated that there are 125,000 retail self-serve machines, and the average cost of the required software changes would be approximately $60 per unit.

There would not be any requirement to change the cash drawers for this accommodation.

8.4.1.2.5. Transportation

The industry representatives estimated that only software modifications would be required for most equipment to accommodate notes with raised tactile features. Based on input from a range of OEMs and transit community association personnel, the ARINC team estimated that the average unit cost of the required software changes would be approximately $60 for each of the estimated 60,000 machines.

Table 8-4. Economic Analysis of Raised Tactile Feature Notes (FY 2009 $M)

Organization/ Market Sector	Nonrecurring Cost	Recurring Annual Cost
BEP	$94.5	$11.9
FRB	$28.0	N/A
High Speed - Desktop	$69.2	$0.0
High Speed - Currency Sorting	$0.4	$0.0
Banking	$1,377.0	$4,722.9
ATM	$24.0	$0.0
Vending	$235.2	$0.0
Retail	$7.5	$0.0
Transportation	$3.6	$0.0
Gaming	$51.0	$0.0
TOTAL	**$1,890.4**	**$4,734.8**

8.4.1.2.6. Gaming

Based on discussions with OEMs, the estimated cost to upgrade software to accept raised tactile features was approximately $60 per machine (all estimated 850,000 machines). The OEM representatives estimated that a hardware change would not be needed.

8.4.1.3. U.S. Individuals

The ARINC team did not identify any direct costs to the general U.S. population resulting from the introduction of raised tactile features.

8.4.1.4. Cost Analysis Summary

Table 8-4 shows a summary of the economic analysis of raised tactile features.

8.4.2. Benefit Analysis

Raised profile features, including dots and bars, could address the key usage scenarios (i.e., quick inventory and public transactions) for blind people. As described in Section 4 of this report, over one half of the survey respondents said that they believed a tactile accommodation would be beneficial. Raised profile tactile features, including raised dots and numerals, have been introduced in Canada. The usability test results in Section 6 of this report indicated the raised dot tactile features, evaluated in tests using new Canadian notes, had the highest average accuracy score (84%) across all existing currency for blind participants (the prototype notches had an average accuracy score of 89%). However, the speed at which participants identified denominations was slower than other accommodations, primarily because participants had difficulty locating the tactile features. In addition, the accuracy rate dropped to 49% for older notes that exhibited wear. Based on these results, the benefit of increased accuracy for this accommodation could be offset by the disadvantages of decreased performance as the note wears, unless a solution for a more durable feature is developed. This could be offset by more frequent removal of widely circulated notes from circulation, however, a higher shred rate would have a significant cost impact, and would increase the number of replacement notes needed from BEP. Development of a more durable method of incorporating raised tactile features could address such issues with raised tactile features.

8.4.3. Other Considerations
Although the study did not investigate the impact of raised tactile features on the general U.S. population, the features tested would not present a major departure from current U.S. currency because they could be incorporated with existing visual designs.

Individuals who use currency readers could be adversely affected by raised tactile features, depending on whether or not the features affect the area of the note used by the device to identify denominations. People with tactile sensitivity impairments may not be able to perceive a tactile feature, and thus would still require a device. Current owners of reader devices could be required to replace or upgrade them to work with physical tactile features.

8.4.4. Conclusions – Raised Tactile Features
The ARINC team performed a cost analysis and a qualitative benefit analysis of raised tactile features as an accommodation for currency denomination by blind people.

- The ARINC team estimated combined Government and industry costs of more than $6.6 billion for initial nonrecurring investment and first-year recurring costs.
- Usability testing of raised dots and intaglio printed bars showed the benefits of raised tactile features, but also highlighted the problems with identifying them on widely circulated notes. In these tests (see Section 6.5), blind participants were able to use the tactile feature to denominate new Canadian notes and the new intaglio printed bars accurately (average of 84% and 85%, respectively). However, recognition accuracy for widely circulated notes was reduced to 49% for the Canadian notes and 42% for the intaglio printed bars.

8.5. Economic Analysis Results: Embedded Tactile Features (strip/patch)

For purposes of this study, the ARINC team (with the approval of the BEP) investigated embedded tactile features as similar to the foil patches that are used in international currencies such as the Canadian dollar, UK pound, and the euro.

8.5.1. Cost Analysis
Table 8-5 in Section 8.5.1.4 provides a summary of the costs for each organization or market sector discussed below. Sections 8.5.1.1 through 8.5.1.3 provide the assumptions specific to the embedded tactile feature accommodation.

8.5.1.1. U.S. Government
An embedded tactile feature would require the BEP to purchase paper from Crane & Co., Inc. with this feature already added; resulting in increased paper costs over what the BEP currently incurs. However, no new equipment unique to generating this feature would be needed.

The incorporation of the embedded feature would result in the generation of additional spoilage during the production process, increasing the overall cost of existing raw materials (paper and ink). The complexity of producing notes increases as more features are added to the production process, increasing the likelihood of spoilage. The spoilage increase would require additional production shifts at all operations. As overall yield declines, more sheets would need to be printed to meet the FRB's currency order requirements.

The initial nonrecurring cost to implement an embedded tactile feature would be approximately $85.2 million. The resulting increase in BEP annual recurring costs would be approximately $57.7 million per year.

The FRB estimated that this type of feature would require sensor software and/or hardware modifications to verify that the correct feature is present and usable. The anticipated sensor software and minor hardware modifications could cost up to $3 million and take up to one year to implement. If a current sensor could not be modified, a new sensor would need to be acquired, which could cost up to $28 million and take four years to develop and deploy. This is the cost reflected in Table 8-4 as the most likely scenario. A hardware change could take two years to implement.

8.5.1.2. U.S. Market Sectors

8.5.1.2.1. High-Speed Machines

One of the top three OEMs (in terms of market share) for high-speed cash processing machines provided quantity and cost estimates for high-speed machines (approximately 230,573 desktop processing machines and 1,383 currency sorting machines). They estimated that for an embedded tactile feature, only a software change would be required for the desktop and currency sorting machines, at approximately $300 per machine.

8.5.1.2.2. Banking/ATM

Commercial banking representatives estimated that the nonrecurring cost drivers for embedded features would be training of tellers, minimal software modifications to cash discriminator equipment, and retooling of automated high-speed processing equipment. The total estimated nonrecurring cost for hardware and software changes for approximately 7,400 banks was estimated to be $6.2 million. The commercial banking representatives estimated no significant impact on annual recurring cost.

The estimated cost to upgrade the estimated 400,000 ATMs for an embedded tactile feature was approximately $60 per machine for software updates. No hardware changes were estimated to be required.

8.5.1.2.3. Vending

Industry representatives provided general information from across the end-user industries with respect to cash-handling equipment. The industry representatives reported that only software modifications would be required for most equipment to accommodate notes with embedded tactile features. Based on input from a range of OEMs and vending community members, the ARINC team estimated that there are approximately 3.92 million units in the U.S. that accept notes in denominations greater than $1 and that the average unit cost of the required software changes would be approximately $60.

8.5.1.2.4. Retail

Based on input from a range of OEMs and retail community members, the ARINC team estimated that there are 125,000 retail self-serve machines and that the average cost of the required software changes would be approximately $60 per unit.

There would not be any requirement to change the cash drawers for this accommodation.

8.5.1.2.5. Transportation

The industry representatives estimated that only software modifications would be required for most equipment to accommodate notes with embedded tactile features. Based on input from a range of OEMs and transit community association personnel, the ARINC team estimated that the average unit cost of the required software changes would be approximately $60 for each of the estimated 60,000 machines.

8.5.1.2.6. Gaming

Based on discussions with OEMs, the estimated cost to upgrade the software to accept embedded tactile features was approximately $60 per machine (all estimated 850,000 machines). The OEM representatives estimated that no hardware change would be needed.

8.5.1.3. U.S. Individuals

The ARINC team did not identify any direct costs to the general U.S. population resulting from the introduction of embedded tactile features.

8.5.1.4. Cost Analysis Summary

Table 8-5 shows a summary of the economic analysis of embedded tactile features.

8.5.2. Benefit Analysis

The ARINC team assessed the benefits of embedded tactile features such as strips or foil patches for the denomination of currency. As described in Section 4 of this report, over one half of the survey respondents said that they believed a tactile accommodation would be beneficial. Three currencies with foil strips and/or foil patches were tested in usability tests (i.e., Canadian dollar, UK pound, and the euro). The test participants found that the Canadian dollar was the only currency where the embedded foil was of any benefit in identifying the denomination of the note. Some participants were able to use the foil strip in the Canadian notes to locate the geometric raised dots as a discriminator, depending on their tactile sensitivity. Participants found that it was much easier to detect the foil on new notes than on widely circulated notes.

Blind participants had difficulty locating the foil patches on both the UK pound and euro notes. The foil patches were of minimal value to the blind participants in determining the denomination. Usability test participants also found that a blank (i.e., little or no ink) area of the paper felt very similar in smoothness to a foil patch. Australian notes include transparent windows with shapes that varied with denomination. These embedded tactile features were not detectable by most of the blind participants.

The testing results did not provide a clear determination of whether embedded tactile features would satisfy the requirements of the primary user scenarios. Enhancements to existing embedded features would be required to make this a viable benefit.

8.5.3. Other Considerations

The ARINC team estimated that the impact on the general U.S. population of an embedded strip or foil patch would not present a major departure from current U.S. currency. As a result, the ARINC team estimated that the implementation impacts would be similar to recent U.S. note redesigns.

Table 8-5. Economic Analysis of Embedded Tactile Feature Notes (FY 2009 $M)

Organization/Market Sector	Nonrecurring Cost	Recurring Annual Cost
BEP	$85.2	$57.7
FRB	$28.0	N/A
High Speed - Desktop	$69.2	$0.0
High Speed - Currency Sorting	$0.4	$0.0
Banking	$6.2	$0.0
ATM	$24.0	$0.0
Vending	$235.2	$0.0
Retail	$7.5	$0.0
Transportation	$3.6	$0.0
Gaming	$51.0	$0.0
TOTAL	**$510.3**	**$57.7**

Individuals who use currency readers could be adversely affected by embedded features, dependent on whether or not the features affect the area of the note used by the device to identify denominations. People with tactile sensitivity impairments may not be able to perceive a tactile feature, and thus would still require a device. Current owners of reader devices could be required to replace or upgrade them to work with physical tactile features.

As described in Section 7.3, major cash machine OEMs (in terms of market share) indicate that significant modification or equipment replacement could be required if the image were changed as a result of placement of embedded tactile features that change the optical design.

8.5.4. Conclusions – Embedded Tactile Features

The ARINC team performed a cost analysis and a qualitative benefit analysis of embedded tactile features as an accommodation for currency denomination by blind people.

- The ARINC team estimated combined Government and industry costs of more than $568 million for nonrecurring investment and first-year recurring costs.
- Embedded tactile features are of limited benefit because they are typically difficult for blind people to locate. Enhancements to existing embedded features would be required in order to make embedded features a viable option for currency denomination.

8.6. Economic Analysis Results: Machine-Readable Features

For purposes of this study, the ARINC team (with the approval of the BEP) investigated overt machine-readable features as a coding methodology feature that could be developed to be readily identified by a device, similar to the feature in the Canadian notes (used by a reader device to identify note denomination).

8.6.1. Cost Analysis

Table 8-6 in Section 8.6.1.4 provides a summary of the costs for each organization or market sector discussed below. Sections 8.6.1.1 through 8.6.1.3 provide the assumptions specific to the machine-readable feature accommodation.

8.6.1.1. U.S. Government

A machine-readable feature would require the BEP to purchase additional inks that would be used as the medium to incorporate this feature. The BEP's existing equipment could be used to print and process this feature. As a result, no new equipment would be required to produce this feature. Due to the physical nature of this feature, the BEP estimated that there should be no negative impact on existing production rates for the various operations. As a result, no increase in production shifts due to a production rate reduction would be expected.

The initial nonrecurring cost to the government to implement an ink-based machine-readable feature would be approximately $70 million for research and development and public education. The resulting increase in BEP annual recurring costs would be approximately $2.8 million per year.

The FRB estimated that implementation of machine-readable features would require minor software and hardware modifications, which could cost as much as $3 million and take one year to develop and deploy.

8.6.1.2. U.S. Market Sectors

Commercial banking representatives estimated that the additional cost of overt machine-readable features would be for training of tellers, which would be similar to the cost for any typical currency redesign. Therefore there are no additional costs estimated as a result of adding this feature to U.S. currency. They also estimated that there would not be significant recurring costs or additional cost for ATMs.

Major OEMs (in terms of market share) did not anticipate a significant cost impact from the addition of machine-readable features to their equipment. The OEMs representatives did not identify a specific cost value, but said that the cost would be similar to what they have experienced for other recent currency design changes.

End-user industry representatives provided general information, but no cost estimates, with respect to cash-handling equipment. The industry representatives reported that no additional major software or hardware changes would be required for most equipment to accommodate notes with machine-readable features.

8.6.1.3. U.S. Individuals

The ARINC team did not identify any direct costs to the general U.S. population resulting from the introduction of machine-readable features.

8.6.1.4. Cost Analysis Summary

Table 8-6 shows a summary of the economic analysis of overt machine-readable features.

8.6.2. Benefit Analysis

The ARINC team assessed the benefits of the addition of machine-readable features to currency. Adding machine-readable features could encourage and facilitate development of new technology currency reader devices. Manufacturers of current devices did not provide information on how their devices work or which specific parameters of notes the devices used for detection.

The currency reader device distributed by the Canadian government is the only portable device whose manufacturer acknowledged employing a machine-readable feature (a coding methodology) to denominate currency. While no comparative data specific to machine-readable features of other currencies was identified, the Canadian device was part of the overall usability testing and the accuracy and speed data for the device were included in this study.

8.6.3. Other Considerations

The results of ARINC team discussions with manufacturers and developers of reader device technology indicated that the unknown size of the commercial market (number of potential customers) is the major constraint for commercial development of such devices.

As described in Section 7.3, major cash machine OEMs (in terms of market share) indicated that significant modification or equipment replacement could be required if the image were changed as a result of placement of overt machine-readable features that change the optical design.

8.6.4. Conclusions – Machine-Readable Features

The ARINC team performed a cost analysis and a qualitative benefit analysis of overt machine- readable features as an accommodation for currency denomination by blind people.

- The ARINC team estimated combined Government and industry costs of more than $75.8 million for initial nonrecurring investment and first-year recurring costs.

8.7. Economic Analysis for Currency Reader Devices

The ARINC team investigated the costs and benefits of currency reader devices, both off-the- shelf devices and prototypes in development. In some cases, the functionality and reliability of prototype devices may be significantly different in the final commercial versions because these prototypes are still undergoing design modifications. However, the ARINC team has included them in this study to illustrate the range of technologies that are possible and to provide examples of the potential impact of new technology developments.

8.7.1. Cost Analysis

Unit prices were readily available for the off-the-shelf devices, as shown in Table 8-7. For the prototypes, the manufacturers provided an estimated cost, but emphasized that the final price would change based on design changes or estimated market size.

The ARINC team investigated the cost of repairs and software upgrades for reader devices. The manufacturer of Slide-in #1 estimated an average repair cost of $50. Slide-in #2 is not functional with U.S. currency; however the manufacturer provided a rough estimated equivalent unit cost in U.S. dollars. The manufacturer of prototype cell phone #2 estimated that, because their product is software, their technology could be hosted on a variety of platforms and that the user would simply purchase a new version of the software whenever updates were needed. The manufacturers of the other devices have not yet established a specific upgrade or repair policy.

8.7.2. Benefit Analysis

The ARINC team assessed the benefits of three commercially available off-the-shelf devices, two operated via insertion of the note into a slot and one operated via cell phone camera platform. The team also tested three prototype devices currently in development, two operated via insertion of the note into a slot and one operated via cell phone camera platform.

Test participants cited portability and speed of use as the most important factors in their willingness to use a reader device. The range of devices tested indicates that device portability is being addressed in several of the device designs, which are smaller than earlier currency readers. Other key factors influencing the use of devices were ease of carrying the device, speed of use (e.g., ease of note insertion and the responsiveness of the device), and social pressure to complete transactions quickly.

Table 8-6. Economic Analysis of Machine-Readable Feature Notes (FY 2009 $M)

Organization/Market Sector	Nonrecurring Cost	Recurring Annual Cost
BEP	$70.0	$2.8
FRB	$3.0	N/A
High Speed - Desktop	$0.0	$0.0
High Speed - Currency Sorting	$0.0	$0.0
Banking	$0.0	$0.0
ATM	$0.0	$0.0
Vending	$0.0	$0.0
Retail	$0.0	$0.0
Transportation	$0.0	$0.0
Gaming	$0.0	$0.0
TOTAL	$73.0	$2.8

The tested devices had a wide range of speed and accuracy results. False positive (inaccurate denomination given) readings were rare; all devices had a less than 1% false positive rate. The most frequent error was a "cannot read" error. Section 6.2.7 provided the detailed results of the usability testing summarized below.

Table 8-7. Reader Device Estimated Unit Costs (FY 2009 $)

| Cost Element | Reader Device Costs | | | | | |
| | Commercially Available* | | | Prototypes ** | | |
	Slide-In #1	Slide-In #2	Cell Phone #1	Slide-In #3	Note Corner Reader	Cell Phone #2
Device Purchase	$330	$120	$1,600	$100	$100	$30
Upgrade for New Currency Design	$50	n/a	n/a	n/a	n/a	$30
Repair	n/a	n/a	n/a	n/a	n/a	$30

* These are currently available, pricing is realistic.
** These are developmental, pricing is uncertain. n/a = data not available from manufacturer.

The usability testing of two commercial slide-in readers (devices #1 and #2) and the prototype slide-in #3 indicated that these devices would provide the greatest benefit among the tested devices. These devices were easiest for the test participants to use and were very accurate (98% to 99% accuracy). Participants correctly identified the currency denomination in approximately 17 seconds using Slide-in #2 and Slide-in #3, and 22 seconds using Slide-in #1. Most participants said they would use these devices at home. Participants routinely commented that they would use the prototype Slide-in #3 for transactions while in line (much more than the other devices tested).

The usability testing of the commercial cell phone note reader (Cell Phone #1) indicated only moderate benefit. The device was moderately easy to use for most participants, but provided the slowest denomination results among the commercial devices. The device correctly denominated the note in an average of 34 seconds. Test participants said that this device would be too slow for use in public, but might be useful for home use because of its very high accuracy rate (100%).

The usability testing of the prototype note corner reader indicated that the current configuration of the device was of marginal benefit to blind test participants. The accuracy (average of 81%) was not as good as the other devices (with the exception of the prototype cell phone device) and the denomination speed (average of 36 seconds) was slower than the commercial devices and prototype slide-in reader. Most participants said they would not use this device, even at home.

The usability testing of the prototype cell-phone reader (Cell Phone #2 Prototype) indicated that the device version tested provided little benefit to blind participants. The device was difficult to use, in some cases taking several minutes to correctly identify a denomination. The low accuracy rate of 76% was primarily a result of participants giving up after several minutes of not being able to get the device to identify a note.

Most blind and VI participants indicated that they do not use a currency reader device (see Section 4.2.2), whether for work (76% never), home (67% never), or when they go out (83% never) and would be reluctant to use reader devices if they had one (e.g., only 36% of survey participants responded that they would use a reader device either occasionally or frequently).

The type of device output (tone, voice, or vibration) was an important consideration for many blind people. Although notification is required to inform the user of the note's denomination, participants cited concerns about a voice output revealing the value of the currency they are carrying to bystanders. Several participants indicated that having the option of an earphone or wireless notification option would be a potential benefit in that people around them would not hear a verbal notification of the value of the currency.

8.7.3. Other Considerations

The ARINC team conducted usability testing on currency reader devices that were operational during the time period between June 2008 and April 2009. The reader device industry continues to introduce new devices to the marketplace as technological breakthroughs are realized. Consumer electronics advance through their product lifecycles (from introduction through maturity to obsolescence) at a rapid rate. When new technology is introduced in commercial products, procurement or acquisition costs are often initially high and then decrease as the product matures in the market. Classic examples are advances in cell phones, personal digital assistants, and GPS equipment.

8.7.4. Conclusions – Currency Reader Devices

The ARINC team performed a cost analysis and a qualitative benefit analysis of six reader devices (three commercial and three prototype devices) to assess their efficacy as an accommodation for currency denomination by blind people. The prototype devices were included in order to provide examples of the potential impact of new technology developments. For the prototypes, the manufacturers provided an estimated cost, but emphasized that the final price would change based on design changes or estimated market size. Section 6.2.7 provided the detailed results from the usability testing summarized below.

- Slide-in note readers provided the greatest benefit among the tested devices. These devices were easiest for the test participants to learn and use and were very accurate (98% to 99% accuracy) in relatively short times (average of between 17 and 21 seconds). The estimated purchase price of these devices ranged from $100 to $330.
- The commercial cell phone reader device provided only moderate benefit to blind test participants, primarily because the denomination time (average of 34 seconds) was slower than the slide-in devices. The estimated purchase price of the device was $1,600, but this device provides other applications in addition to currency identification.
- The prototype note corner reader was of marginal benefit to the blind test participants because the device accuracy (average 81%) was lower and the denomination speed (average of 36 seconds) slower than the other devices tested. The estimated purchase price of the device was $100.
- The prototype cell phone device was too difficult for the blind test participants to use to be beneficial. Although this device had the lowest estimated price ($30), that would be for the software only, the cost of a platform cell phone was not included.

8.8. Economic Analysis Conclusions

Table 8-8 presents the summary cost for each currency feature studied. As mentioned in Section 7.1, these are the costs that were available during the time period of this study. Further data collection and analysis could provide additional granularity. The ARINC team conducted sensitivity analyses, varying some of the uncertain elements. Changing the inputs over a range of costs did not change the results of the cost analysis (i.e., the relative magnitude of estimated costs as compared between accommodations). The ARINC team anticipated that this relative magnitude of the differences between the accommodations would not change significantly unless a significant technological advance radically alters the considerations for a particular accommodation. Thus, the ARINC team believes that these costs analyses provide a solid basis for comparison among alternatives.

9. CONCLUSION

This section provides a summary of the conclusions presented in each of the preceding sections.

The ARINC team identified currency user requirements and needs of blind and VI people, evaluated the practical implementation considerations of various currency features, and measured the effectiveness of features that have been implemented worldwide. The ARINC team developed conclusions related to the demographics of the blind and VI communities, focus group results, survey results, technical analysis of accommodations, usability test results, and economic analysis results. This section provides a summary of all the conclusions of this study.

9.1. Blind and VI Communities

For the purposes of this study, the ARINC team used the following definitions:

- **Blind** = people who have no useful vision for reading any amount of print.
- **Visually Impaired** = people who have difficulty seeing but have some useful vision, defined for this study as being able to read some print (with or without corrective lenses).

These definitions were supported by the ARINC team experience in focus groups and with usability test participants. All of the focus group and usability participants who said they had some useful vision could denominate U.S. currency in a room with normal lighting, although a few required magnification or a special lens.

Based on available population studies and using the established definitions, the ARINC team estimated that in 2008 there were 304,060 blind people and 4,067,309 VI people in the U.S. Based on U.S. Government population growth estimates, the ARINC team projects that by 2020, there will be 340,547 blind people and 4,555,386 VI people in the U.S.

Table 8-8. Summary Cost per Accommodation (FY 2009 $M)

Accommodation	Nonrecurring Cost	Recurring Annual Cost	Total 1st Year Cost
1-D Size Change	$5,131.4	$4,388.6	$9,520.0
2-D Size Change	$6,189.3	$4,421.6	$10,610.9
Mechanical Tactile	$1,894.4	$4,731.3	$6,625.7
Raised Tactile	$1,890.4	$4,734.8	$6,625.2
Embedded Tactile	$510.3	$57.7	$568.0
Machine-Readable	$73.0	$2.8	$75.8

9.2. Focus Group Results

More than one hundred blind and VI people participated in focus group sessions, including open forum discussions and small group sessions, to provide information about their experience with the use of U.S. currency. The following conclusions result from the focus group sessions:

- Three currency usage scenarios were the most important to participants: (1) transactions with no other people in close proximity, (2) transactions while in line (with people waiting), and (3) quick inventory of wallet or purse.
- Existing challenges for blind and VI people in the use of U.S. currency include (1) receiving the wrong denomination in change or providing the wrong denomination in a transaction, (2) social stigma caused by the time required for them to correctly identify a currency denomination, and (3) the potential for problems inherent in interactions with strangers.
- Adaptations to cope with existing currency for transactions include (1) sorting notes beforehand, (2) using sighted assistance after the transaction, (3) use of electronic note identifiers, and (4) choosing non-cash transactions.

The information gathered in the focus group sessions was used to develop a survey to characterize vision-related difficulties with currency and to gain an understanding of how various currency accommodations might meet the needs of the blind and VI participants.

9.3. Survey Results

The ARINC team conducted a survey to explore vision-related issues with U.S. currency. The survey was administered to 402 participants, 196 VI people and 206 blind people, with a broad geographic and demographic range. The survey yielded conclusions in the following areas:

Participant behavior:

- Survey respondents are active participants in the economy; they use computers regularly (95%), are active in their communities (90%), and work (88%).
- Respondents most-frequently used the $1 currency denomination, followed by the $5, $20, and $10 denominations.
- Respondents typically use a wide variety of technological devices, including cell phones (89%), computer screen reader (86%), and flatbed scanners (69%).
- Respondents rarely use currency readers at work (76% never), home (67% never), or in public (83% never).
- When asked if they had a reader device, would they take it with them when they go out in public, 36% of respondents said that they would (27% occasionally, 9% frequently), 23% said rarely, while 41% said they would never take a device with them.

Primary concerns with currency use:

- Survey respondents feel rushed during transactions (72%).
- Respondents feel vulnerable using cash (70%).
- Respondents used incorrect denominations in a transaction within the past year (62%).
- Respondents rely on someone at the point of sale to tell them what denominations they were receiving (59%).

Accommodations:

- There was nearly the same percentage of participants who suggested a tactile accommodation (53%) as there was that suggested note size differences (52%).

9.4. Analysis of Accommodations

The ARINC team performed a technical analysis focused on the practical implementation of currency features for blind and VI people. Five major features were analyzed:

- Numeral size changes are a proven means to address quick inventory and public transaction scenarios for VI people.
- Primary color changes for different denominations are options to address quick inventory and public transaction scenarios for VI people. While predominant color changes may be of value for a subset of the VI population, increasing the contrast of features, such as numerals, would be of greater benefit.
- Notches on the long edges of notes were readily and quickly detectable by all participants who were tested. However, some potential users may still have difficulty perceiving the feature, or with remembering the value encoding system. The introduction of tactile features such as perforations or notched edges in the

manufacturing process could cause surface contamination that could adversely affect downstream processing.

- Raised profile tactile features, including raised dots and intaglio bars, were effective when new, especially for those who are blind. However these tactile features were found to lose some of their effectiveness on widely circulated notes. Industrial users and manufacturers are concerned with the effect of raised features on stacking, mechanical counting examination, and finishing processes.
- A number of countries (e.g., including the UK, Sweden, Switzerland, and Australia) and the EU vary note size by denomination as an accommodation for blind and VI people. Introduction of size changes without an existing infrastructure would require significantly modified hardware for counting and authentication at every step where these devices are employed in both Government and commercial processes.

The ARINC team also looked at currency reader devices as a potential accommodation for both blind and VI people. Survey respondents, however, were split about whether they would consider using the devices: over 36% said they would, either occasionally or frequently, while 41% said they never would. The type of device output (tone, voice, vibration) is an important consideration for blind and VI people to address concerns about the device revealing the value of their currency to people nearby. Portability and speed of use are the critical factors in the willingness of blind and VI people to use a reader device.

9.5. Usability Testing

The ARINC team conducted usability testing to measure how well the various accessibility accommodations accomplish their intended purpose. Usability was measured in terms of speed to denominate currency and the accuracy of the recognition for blind and VI participants.

In general the results of usability tests showed that:

- None of the tested accommodations would enable all blind or VI people to distinguish denominations in the key scenarios 100% of the time, without feeling rushed.
- For both blind and VI people, a combination of complementary features could result in satisfactory results in the key usage scenarios.
- Most participants cited three of the currency features that address the needs of both blind and VI people (i.e., notches, raised tactile features, and size changes), as viable solutions.

9.5.1. Device Usability Testing

The ARINC team performed usability testing on six currency reader devices that were available at the time of the usability testing, between June 2008 and April 2009. The ARINC team measured usability of reader devices in terms of speed to denominate currency and time to learn to use the device for blind and VI participants.

- Slide-in #1 was easy for the test participants to learn and use. This device had an average training time of 183 seconds and average speed to accurately denominate notes of 21.7 seconds. The device error rate increased as battery power decreased, but infrequent errors still occurred even with fresh batteries. Participants said that the device was too large to carry with them for public transactions.
- Slide-in #2 was easy for the test participants to learn and use. The device had an average first-use training time of 140 seconds and correctly denominated the note in an average time of 17.3 seconds. Test participants said that the portability and switchable output modes were preferred over Slide-in #1.
- Slide-in #3 was the most portable device and was easy enough to learn and use for most participants, but not for participants who had dexterity impairments. The device had an average first-use training time of 177 seconds and correctly denominated the note in an average time of 17.6 seconds.
- Cell phone #1 was moderately easy to use for most participants, but was relatively slow. The device had an average training time of 251 seconds and correctly denominated the note in an average of 34.2 seconds. Test participants said that this device would be too slow for use in public, but might be useful at home.
- Cell phone #2 was difficult to use for participants, and was slowest among the devices tested. The device had an average training time of 319 seconds and correctly denominated the note in an average of 102.5 seconds.
- The note corner reader device had an average training time of 201 seconds and correctly denominated the note in an average time of 36.5 seconds.

9.5.2. Usability Testing of U.S. and Foreign Currency

The ARINC team conducted usability testing for U.S. currency and a range of foreign currency. The purpose of these tests was to establish the effectiveness of different features that have been implemented in the various currency designs.

9.5.2.1. U.S. Dollars

U.S. dollars have the following features that assist the VI community: (1) large, high-contrast numerals ($5, $10, $20, and $50 notes); (2) large portraits that vary by denomination; and (3) subtle background color that varies by denomination. The ARINC team developed the following conclusions:

- Both the notes with no background color and the later generation notes with background color were identifiable over 94% of the time by VI participants, if held close enough to the eye.
- The light/dark silhouette (portrait) of each denomination and strong foreground/ background color contrast of U.S. currency aids recognition for VI participants.
- The large purple numeral on the redesigned $5 note was more helpful in the usability tests than the enlarged numerals on the $10, $20, and $50 notes.
- With the exception of the $5 note, VI participants found that denominating notes with the new background color was slower on average than with the older designs without the background color.

- VI participants said that $50 notes and $20 notes are easy to confuse, because the 5 and 2 numerals look similar. This effect was noted with other currencies.
- VI participants said that they would prefer that the primary large numbers for denominating notes be located in the upper left corner, instead of the lower right corner to enable quicker denomination without removing the notes from a wallet.
- The $100 note, which does not have the larger high contrast numeral, was the most difficult for VI participants to recognize, taking approximately twice as long for VI test participants to recognize.

9.5.2.2. UK Pounds

UK pounds have the following features for the blind and VI communities: (1) size variation, proportionally in two dimensions, with denomination; (2) primary color variation with denomination; (3) large-print numerals (except the £50 note) and smaller high-contrast numerals (except the newer £20 note); (4) a graphic geometric pattern on each note (except the new £20 note); and (5) a foil patch (£20 and £50 notes) or foil strip (£10 and £5 notes). The ARINC team developed the following conclusions:

- The largest (£50) and smallest (£5) UK notes had the highest accuracy denomination success rates for blind participants (90% and 57%, respectively).
- Blind participants found it difficult to find the foil patches on the notes. Once they located the patches, blind participants found the foil patches difficult to differentiate.
- VI participants were able to identify UK pound denominations with an average accuracy of 90%.
- The numerals on the £50 note were more difficult for VI participants to read than on any of the other denominations. While this did not significantly affect VI participants' accuracy (93%), it did increase the average time required for denomination.

9.5.2.3. Euros

Euros have the following features for the blind and VI communities: (1) size variation, proportionally in two dimensions, with denomination; (2) large-print numerals; (3) high-contrast numerals; (4) dramatic base color differences between denominations; and (5) a foil strip along the left side of the front (€5, €10, and €20 notes) or foil patches on the right side of the front (€50 and €100 notes). The ARINC team developed the following conclusions:

- Blind participants recognized the €5 note 87% of the time, more accurately than the other denominations (ranged from 51% to 57%).
- Blind participants incorrectly denominated euros when they confused one denomination with the next-higher or next-lower denomination because it was hard for them to perceive the small size differences between denominations.
- VI people were able to denominate euros quickly (4.7–6.3 seconds) and accurately (88%–97%).
- The primary large print numerals on the front of the note were easily visible for VI participants.
- The €5 note was recognizable primarily by the small note size.

9.5.2.4. Swedish Kronor

Swedish kronor have the following features for the blind and VI communities: (1) size variation independently in two dimensions with denomination and (2) color variation with denomination. The ARINC team developed the following conclusions:

- The recognition accuracy of between 52% and 91% was better for kronor than for other currencies using size differential accommodation. As with other size-based formats, the largest and smallest denominations were the most accurately recognized by blind participants.
- VI participants were able to denominate kronor quickly (5.4–7.1 seconds) and accurately (99–100%).

9.5.2.5. Swiss Francs

Swiss francs have the following features for the blind and VI communities: (1) length variation with denomination; (2) stark color variation with denomination; and (3) high-contrast numerals. The ARINC team developed the following conclusions:

- Blind participants were able to denominate Swiss francs with accuracy scores between 54% and 78%.
- VI participants most often relied on the numerals for denomination of the notes, rather than relying on the base color differences.
- VI test participants were able to correctly denominate the Swiss franc between 87% and 95% of the time, with an approximately five percentage point lower accuracy for the CHF20 and CHF50 denominations.

9.5.2.6. Australian Dollars

Australian dollars have the following features for the blind and VI communities: (1) length variation with denomination; (2) distinct base color variation with denomination; (3) polypropylene polymer substrate with a transparent plastic window embedded in one corner; and (4) large-print numerals. The ARINC team developed the following conclusions:

- Blind participants were able to denominate Australian notes (7mm length increments) an average of 17 percentage points less accurately than Swiss notes (11mm length increments).
- The stark base color differences and the size and clarity of the type used for the numerals helped VI participants denominate Australian notes quickly (under 6.2 seconds) and accurately (98–100%).

9.5.2.7. Canadian Dollars

Canadian dollars have the following features for the blind and VI communities: (1) base color variation with denomination; (2) a tactile feature consisting of a pattern of clustered raised dots; (3) a foil strip along the left side of the notes; and (4) large-print, high-contrast numerals. The ARINC team developed the following conclusions:

- Blind participants were able to use the tactile feature, consisting of a pattern of clustered raised dots, to denominate new Canadian notes accurately, identifying between 82% and 93% of the notes correctly, depending on denomination.
- Recognition accuracy for widely circulated notes was reduced significantly for blind participants.
- The time required for blind participants to identify denominations was relatively high due primarily to difficulty locating the tactile features.
- VI participants were able to denominate Canadian notes quickly (within an average of 4.4 to 6.5 seconds for all denominations) and accurately (greater than 96% for all denominations), primarily using the large-print numerals.

9.5.3. Usability Testing of Prototype Currency Accommodations

The ARINC team conducted usability testing for a series of prototype sample test sets representative of currency accommodations for blind people. The purpose of these tests was to establish the effectiveness of different accommodations that could be implemented in future currency designs. Prototype sample test sets were tested with four features: tactile notch features, one-dimensional (length) size variation (1-D), two dimensional (length and width) size variation (2-D), and printed tactile bar features.

9.5.3.1. Notches

Usability test participants found that denominating notes using notched edges was relatively accurate (average of 89%) and quick (average of 8.5 seconds) for participants. These results were comparable to the most effective international currencies, i.e., higher accuracy than the Canadian dollar (new) and slightly slower than the Swedish kronor and Swiss franc.

9.5.3.2. 1-D Sizes

1-D sizes varied in length only, with 4 or 5 mm increments in length with each denomination. Lengths varied from 156 mm for a $1 note to 180 mm for a $100 note. All participants found this system difficult to use accurately. Because participants had low confidence in their perception of small size differences, participants guessed quickly (an average speed value of approximately nine seconds) but inaccurately (an average accuracy of 41%).

9.5.3.3. 2-D Sizes

2-D sizes varied in both length and width, with 12 mm differences in length (i.e., three possible lengths, 156 mm, 168 mm, or 180 mm) and 16 mm differences in width (i.e., two possible lengths, 66 mm or 82 mm). Participants found this system moderately easy to use but had difficulty with accurate perception of length differences. Participants had trouble remembering the value assignment system, which added to a perception that this system was cumbersome and relatively difficult. The average speed was fairly slow at 10.7 seconds and the average accuracy was fairly low at 63%.

9.5.3.4. Bars

The prototype bars included heavy intaglio print lines on the far edges of the notes, in the area normally left blank on U.S. notes. Clusters of five thin bars appeared in three different locations, with four possible conditions (zero, one, two, or three clusters). Some participants could detect these clusters fairly accurately (average accuracy of 85%) when they were newly printed (not widely circulated), but detection was relatively slow (average speed of 17.1 seconds).

Participants had much more difficulty detecting the bar features when the prototype notes were moderately circulated. The measured accuracy was reduced to an average of 42%. The added difficulty also made detection slower (average speed of 20.6 seconds).

9.5.4. Overall Usability Test Conclusions

The ARINC team developed the following conclusions from the blind participant usability tests:

- The notched prototype currency resulted in the highest accuracy score (89%) for blind usability test participants. The time required for blind participants to denominate notes with this method was also relatively fast (average of 8.5 seconds).
- Raised dot tactile features, evaluated in tests of new Canadian notes, resulted in a high accuracy score average of 84% (across all denominations) for blind usability test participants. The time required for blind participants to identify denominations was relatively slow (average of 16.2 seconds), due primarily to difficulty locating the tactile features.
- Raised dot tactile features were effective with new notes, but wear of the tactile feature is a significant concern; accuracy scores were reduced from an average of 84% to an average of 49% for notes in widely circulated condition.
- Distinct note size differences (i.e., Swedish kronor) resulted in the highest speed performance for blind usability test participants. Smaller size differences (e.g., UK pound, euro, Australian dollar, Swiss franc, and the prototype 1-D and 2-D sizes), resulted in slower denomination.
- Test participants cited portability and speed of use as the most important factors in their willingness to use a reader device. The key factors described by participants were ease of carrying the device, speed of use, and social pressure to move along quickly.
- Training and familiarity are important for effective use of both tactile and size differences.
- It is unlikely that any single feature tested (or combination of features) will enable all blind and VI people to denominate currency with 100% accuracy in the key scenarios (quick inventory and public transactions) without feeling rushed.

The ARINC team developed the following conclusions from the VI participant usability tests:

- VI usability test participants were able to denominate all of the currencies tested with at least 90% accuracy.

- Currency with large, high-contrast numerals (e.g., from the U.S., Canada, Australia, and Sweden) all showed denomination accuracy above 95%.
- Subtle background color differences like those used in the newer U.S. notes were not useful for VI participants. With the exception of the $5 note, VI participants found that denominating notes with the new background color was slower on average than with the older designs without the background color.

9.6. Economic Analysis

The ARINC team performed an economic analysis of several sample accommodations for blind people. Each example was intended to establish a relevant scope and magnitude of the impact of each accommodation to provide a basis for comparison with the other alternatives. The economic analysis considered the costs as well as the qualitative benefits of each accommodation. Seven categories of accommodations were included in the analysis:

- Size changes along one dimension (1-D)
- Size changes along two dimensions (2-D)
- Mechanical tactile features (notches or perforations)
- Raised tactile features (dots or bars)
- Embedded tactile features (strip or patch)
- Overt machine-readable features (readable by device)
- Currency reader devices

The costs and benefits of the accommodations that were considered included operational and technical impacts; cost to businesses, vendors, banks, and other handlers of currency; and benefits to the blind and VI community in the key usage scenarios. The economic analyses of each of the accommodations are summarized in the following subsections.

9.6.1. Economic Analysis of 1-D Sizes

The ARINC team performed a cost analysis and a qualitative benefit analysis of 1-D sizes (i.e., variation of length by denomination) as an accommodation for currency denomination by blind people. The ARINC team developed the following conclusions:

- The ARINC team estimated combined Government and industry costs of more than $9.5 billion for nonrecurring investment and annual recurring costs for the first year.
- Usability tests of currency with 1-D sizes (i.e., Australian, Swiss, and the Prototype 1-D sizes) indicated that blind participants were able to achieve only moderate denomination accuracy (average ranged between 41% and 65% as shown in Section 6.5), even though the denomination speed was relatively good (average ranged between 7.4 and 12.9 seconds, see Section 6.4). The results were best with the currency having the largest difference between sizes (Swiss), and the worst with the Prototype 1-D sizes, which had the smallest difference between sizes.

9.6.2. Economic Analysis of 2-D Sizes

The ARINC team performed a cost analysis and a qualitative benefit analysis of 2-D sizes as an accommodation for currency denomination by blind people. The ARINC team developed the following conclusions:

- The ARINC team estimated combined Government and industry costs of more than $10.6 billion for nonrecurring investment and annual recurring costs for the first year.
- Distinct two-dimensional note size differences (Swedish kronor) resulted in the best average speed performance (7.2 seconds) and accuracy (78%) for blind usability test participants for all of the currency types with size differences. Smaller size differences (UK pound, euro, and prototype 2-D sizes), resulted in slower speeds (averages ranged between 10.1 and 10.8 seconds) and lower accuracy (averages ranged between 60% and 65%).

9.6.3. Economic Analysis of Mechanical Tactile Features

The ARINC team performed a cost analysis and a qualitative benefit analysis of mechanical tactile features (i.e., notches) as an accommodation for currency denomination by blind people. The ARINC team developed the following conclusions:

- The ARINC team estimated combined Government and industry costs of more than $6.6 billion for nonrecurring investment and annual recurring costs for the first year.
- Blind usability test participants were more accurate at denominating notches than any other currency or feature in this study. Most blind participants were able to denominate the system of notches accurately (average of 89%) and quickly (average of 8.5 seconds).

9.6.4. Economic Analysis of Raised Tactile Features

The ARINC team performed a cost analysis and a qualitative benefit analysis of raised tactile features as an accommodation for currency denomination by blind people. The ARINC team developed the following conclusions:

- The ARINC team estimated combined Government and industry costs of more than $6.6 billion for initial nonrecurring investment and annual recurring costs for the first year.
- Usability testing of raised dots and intaglio printed bars showed the benefits of raised tactile features, but also highlighted the problems with identifying them on widely circulated notes. In these tests, blind participants were able to use the tactile feature to denominate new Canadian notes accurately (average of 84%). The intaglio printed bars had similar results on new notes (average of 85%). However, recognition accuracy for widely circulated notes was greatly reduced for both the raised dots (average of 49%) and the intaglio printed bars (average of 42%).

9.6.5. Economic Analysis of Embedded Tactile Features

The ARINC team performed a cost analysis and a qualitative benefit analysis of embedded tactile features as an accommodation for currency denomination by blind people. The ARINC team developed the following conclusions:

- The ARINC team estimated combined Government and industry costs of more than $568 million for nonrecurring investment and annual recurring costs for the first year.
- Embedded tactile features are of limited benefit because they are typically difficult for blind people to locate. Enhancements to existing embedded features would be required in order to make embedded features a viable option for currency denomination.

9.6.6. Economic Analysis of Machine-Readable Features

The ARINC team performed a cost analysis and a qualitative benefit analysis of overt machine- readable features as an accommodation for currency denomination by blind people. The ARINC team developed the following conclusions:

- The ARINC team estimated Government and industry costs of more than $75.8 million for initial nonrecurring investment and annual recurring costs for the first year.
- Machine-readable features could enable manufacturers to develop new currency reader device technologies that the blind and VI community might be more inclined to use.

9.6.7. Economic Analysis of Currency Reader Devices

The ARINC team performed a cost analysis and a qualitative benefit analysis of six reader devices (three commercial and three prototype devices) to assess their efficacy as an accommodation for currency denomination by blind people. For the prototype devices, the manufacturers provided an estimated cost, but emphasized that the final price would change based on design changes or estimated market size. The ARINC team developed the following conclusions:

- Slide-in note readers provided the greatest benefit among the tested devices. These devices were easiest for the test participants to learn and use and were very accurate (98% to 99% accuracy) in relatively short times (average of between 17.3 and 21.7 seconds). The estimated purchase price of these devices ranged from $100 to $330.
- The commercial cell phone reader device provided only moderate benefit to blind test participants, primarily because the denomination time (average of 34 seconds) was slower than the slide-in devices. The estimated purchase price of the device was $1,600, but this device provides other applications in addition to currency identification.
- The prototype note corner reader was of marginal benefit to the blind test participants because the device accuracy (average 81%) was lower and the denomination speed

(average of 36.5 seconds) slower than the other devices tested (except for the prototype cell phone). The estimated purchase price of the device was $100.

- The prototype cell phone device was too difficult for the blind test participants to use to be beneficial. The estimated price of $30 covers only the software; a cell phone would need to be purchased separately.

10. DECISION MODEL

The ARINC team decision model contains criteria against which the various accommodations were measured, enabling comparison across different accommodations. The decision model includes provisions to factor in a variety of considerations ranging from an accommodation's compatibility with current security features to the convenience of the accommodation on an individual user level.

The ARINC team decision model that was adapted for use in this study was designed to facilitate the determination of the relative value of a set of alternatives. Cost data from the economic analysis in Section 8 could be used to compare with relative benefits and other implications of each accommodation.

The benefits of the decision model tool are that it provides objective metrics (e.g., cost) as well as subjective assessment scores that characterize the impact of subjective (e.g., non-cost) criteria. The decision model also enables documentation and tracking of changes, thus providing a historical record of both judgments and data used in reaching a decision. Finally, the model provides decision makers with a methodology that can accommodate the dynamic nature of emergent or changing criteria, versus a static snapshot of data at only one historical point.

Characteristics of the decision model include:

- Flexibility, in that the scores and criteria used in determining the relative values can be changed as necessary
- Use of individual or team scoring of subjective factors
- Potential to assign different scoring weights to specific individuals such as subject matter experts and key decision makers
- Simplicity, in that only the four basic math functions are employed within the spreadsheet

10.1. Decision Model Framework

The ARINC team established the model framework by determining which alternatives to compare, determining what subjective (non-cost) criteria to analyze, and defining the cost elements to analyze.

The ARINC team developed the alternatives and the subjective criteria based on information from focus groups, surveys, and usability testing in conjunction with analysis by team subject matter experts. The BEP reviewed and approved the alternative accommodations and the criteria to form the framework for the model. Appendix L provides a list of the decision model criteria and definitions.

10.2. Scoring Methodology

The ARINC team used a group consensus approach to scoring, using results of both the usability testing and the economic analysis to inform the process. This method encouraged an open discussion of the criteria and scoring, with key input coming from team members with the most knowledge about the subject area.

Scoring of the criteria is counter-intuitive because **a low score is considered better than a high score**. The model was designed so that alternatives with a lower value had a more positive rating than those with a higher relative value. The subjective ratings were therefore on the same scale as the cost estimates, where an alternative with a lower relative cost (and a parallel lower subjective score) is a more favorable alternative. The cost and subjective criteria ratings were combined for a total overall value for each alternative.

For example, the initial acquisition cost of a piece of equipment could be less than that of an alternative. However, when relative values for such criteria as functionality and security are integrated with total cost, the higher priced equipment could be the preferred alternative. This concept was critical to understanding the model utility because the goal was to determine the relative merits of the alternatives considering the numerous cost and benefit elements that must be reviewed.

10.3. Decision Model Evaluation

Appendix M provides the cost elements and non-cost subjective factors agreed upon by the ARINC team and the BEP for purposes of this study. Appendix M also provides the results of the ARINC team scoring exercise.

End Notes

[1] Denominate is defined as the ability to differentiate the various denominations of U.S. currency.
[2] National Research Council, 1995, Currency Features for Visually Impaired People. National Materials Advisory Board, NRC. Washington D.C.: National Academy Press, ISBN 0-309-05194-0.
[3] National Research Council, 1995, Currency Features for Visually Impaired People. National Materials Advisory Board, NRC. Washington D.C.: National Academy Press, ISBN 0-309-05194-0.
[4] Federal Reserve Bank of St. Louis Review; pp 371-414, September/October (2007)
[5] Steinmetz E., 2006. "Americans with Disabilities: 2002". Household Economic Studies, Current Population Reports (Report No. P70-107). Washington, DC: U.S. Census Bureau. See: http://www.census.gov/prod/2006pubs/p70-107.pdf, page 5. (site checked and available as of 7/20/2009)
[6] Reported by Lighthouse International as Adams, P.F., Hendershot, G.E., & Marano, M.A. (1999). Current estimates from the National Health Interview Survey, 1996. National Center for Health Statistics. Vital Health Statistics, 10 (200). See also http://www.lighthouse.org/research/statistics-on-vision-impairment/references/ (site checked and available as of 7/20/2009)
[7] World Health Organization definition as cited by the World Blind Union at http://www.worldblindunion.org/en/appdocumentos/umc2en/prod/WBU%20Definition%20of%20Blindness.doc. See also World Health Organization http://apps.who.int/classifications/apps/icd/icd10online/gh53.htm, section H54 for more information. (sites checked and available as of 7/20/2009)

[8] SSA Statutory Blindness, http://www.ssa.gov/dibplan/dqua lify8.htm (site checked and available as of 7/20/2009)

[9] Professor of Ophthalmology, Wilmer Eye Institute, personal communication with members of the ARINC team, 12 December 2008

[10] See http://www.preventblindness.org/vpus/2008_update/VPUS_vision_impairment_blindness_2008.pdf *Prevalence of Adult Vision Impairment and Age-Related Eye Disease in America"* pages 4, 6, and 8 (site checked and available as of 7/20/2009)

[11] National Eye Institute Report "Statistics on Blindness in the Model Reporting Area, 1969-70,"(Publication No. [NIH] 73-427 See http://www.eric.ed.gov/ERICWebPortal/custom/portlets/recordDetails/detailmini.jsp?_nfpb=true&_&ERICExtSearch_SearchValue_0=ED082419&ERICExtSearch_SearchType_0=no&accno=ED 082419, choose full text .pdf option. (site checked and available as of 7/20/2009)

[12] National Center for Health Statistics, NHIS-Disability Supplement, 1994 and 1995 (as reported by the American Foundation for the Blind at http://www.afb.org/Section.asp?SectionID=15&DocumentID=4398#legal) "Numbers of Legally Blind Americans" (site checked and available as of 7/20/2009) 13 http://www.census.gov/population/www/pop-profile/profile_list.html -- "Population Profile of the United States: 1995" Highlights -1st bullet (site checked and available as of 7/20/2009)

[13] http://www.census.gov/population/www/pop-profile/profile_list.html -- "Population Profile of the United States: 1995" Highlights -1st bullet (site checked and available as of 7/20/2009)

[14] http://www.census.gov/popest/national/asrh/NC-EST2008/NC-EST2008-01.xls (site checked and available as of 7/20/2009)

[15] See http://www.preventblindness.org/vpus/2008_update/VPUS_vision_impairment_blindness_2008.pdf. *"Prevalence of Adult Vision Impairment and Age-Related Eye Disease in America"* charts on page 5 (site checked and available as of 7/20/2009).

[16] http://www.census.gov/popest/national/asrh/NC-EST2008/NC-EST2008-01.xls (site checked and available as of 7/20/2009)

[17] National Eye Institute, "Report of the Visual Impairment and its Rehabilitation Panel" at www.nei.nih.gov/resources/strategicplans/neiplan/frm_impairment.asp (site checked and available as of 7/20/2009)

[18] http://www.census.gov/popest/national/asrh/NC-EST2008/NC-EST2008-01.xls (site checked and available as of 7/20/2009)

[19] National Eye Institute, "Report of the Visual Impairment and its Rehabilitation Panel" at www.nei.nih.gov/resources/strategicplans/neiplan/frm_impairment.asp (Site checked and available as of 7/20/2009)

[20] Detailed estimates are available at http://www.census.gov/population/www/projections/downloadablefiles.html (Site checked and available as of 7/20/2009)

[21] All ACB and NFB convention participants were invited to attend. Open forum events were advertised in the conference agendas.

[22] National Research Council, 1995, Currency Features for VI People. National Materials Advisory Board, NRC. Washington D.C.: National Academy Press, ISBN 0-309-05194-0.

[23] European Blind Union (EBU). 1994. A Report of the European Blind Union Expert Working Group on Currency: Recommendations for the Design of the ECU. Paris, France: EBU.

[24] National Research Council Committee on Vision. 1980. Recommended standard procedures for the clinical measurement and specification of visual acuity.

[25] Advances in Ophthalmology 41:103-148.

[26] Associate Professor of Optometry, New England College of Optometry, personal communication with members of the ARINC team, 29 July 2008.

[27] Currency Technology Office, Federal Reserve Bank, personal communication with members of the ARINC team, 7 October 2008.

[28] Professor of Optometry, New England College of Optometry, personal communication with members of the ARINC team, 1 October 2008.

[29] Professor of Optometry, University of California at Berkley, personal communication with members of the ARINC team, 3 October 2008.

[30] National Research Council, 1995, Currency Features for Visually Impaired People. National Materials Advisory Board, NRC. Washington D.C.: National Academy Press, ISBN 0-309-05194-0

[31] National Research Council, 1995, Currency Features for Visually Impaired People. National Materials Advisory Board, NRC. Washington D.C.: National Academy Press, ISBN 0-309-05194-0, Appendix D shows 128 of 171 countries vary denominations by size

[32] Lederman, S.J. & Hamilton, C. (2002). Using tactile features to help functionally blind individuals denominate banknotes. Human Factors, 44(3), 413-428. Downloadable at http://psyc.queensu.ca/~cheryl/reprints.html.

[33] Personal communication, FRB Richmond, March 19, 2009.

[34] Supplemental Testimony Statement of Richard M. Geerdes, NCE, President and Chief Executive Officer, National Automatic Merchandising Association. House Financial Services Committee, Subcommittee on Domestic Monetary Policy, Hearing, July 30, 2008

[35] NAMA Ad Hoc Currency Usage Survey, conducted 9/4/08 to 9/10/08 by Thomas McMahon, NAMA Senior V.P & Chief Counsel; and NAMA Bill Acceptor Use Estimate, 4/8/09, by Richard Geerdes, NAMA President and CEO.

[36] Supplemental Testimony Statement of Richard M. Geerdes, NCE, President and Chief Executive Officer, National Automatic Merchandising Association. House Financial Services Committee, Subcommittee on Domestic Monetary Policy, Hearing, July 30, 2008

[37] National Research Council, 1995, Currency Features for VI People. National Materials Advisory Board, NRC. Washington D.C.: National Academy Press, ISBN 0-309-05194-0.

[38] National Research Council, 1995, Currency Features for VI People. National Materials Advisory Board, NRC. Washington D.C.: National Academy Press, ISBN 0-309-05194-0.

INDEX